Yorks
Women's Institute
Cookery Book

MORE THAN 400 TRADITIONAL RECIPES
GATHERED BY MEMBERS OF
THE YORKSHIRE WOMEN'S INSTITUTE

DALESMAN

Dalesman Publishing Company
Stable Courtyard, Broughton Hall,
Skipton, North Yorkshire BD23 3AE

First Edition 1996

Text © Yorkshire Women's Institute 1996
Cover photograph © Peter Williams, taken from Delicious Home
Cooking by Caroline Conran (Conran Octopus)

A British Library Cataloguing in Publication record
is available for this book

ISBN 1 85568 110 2

Printed by Knight & Willson, Leeds

Contents

Introduction

Ever since it was founded in 1897 in Canada (1915 in this country) the Women's Institute has been a cornerstone of rural life for generations of women. Over the years the WI has always been synonymous with thrift, value for money and sound common sense, especially in the kitchen.

This handy and practical cookery book brings together almost a century of culinary wisdom accumulated and handed down by members of the WI in Yorkshire. Within this collection of more than 400 recipes, home baking and traditional household favourites such as Farmhouse Winter Vegetable Pie and Steak and Kidney Pudding mingle with more exotic fare. Iced Cucumber and Yoghurt Soup and Chicken with Apricots and Brandy eloquently demonstrate the way that the Women's Institute and its members have continued to move with the times, catering for increasingly sophisticated tastes and making use of the full range of international ingredients available to the modern cook and demanded by their families.

All are described in an appealingly simple, easy-to-follow style with all the recipes tried and tested by the members themselves in their own kitchens. The collection has been chosen to give the true flavour of Yorkshire with the very best of its popular traditional dishes allied to tasty modern variations to ensure this is true home cooking which will appeal to the modern family.

This compilation was achieved by the close co-operation and diligent application of Anne Harrison (chairman, North Yorkshire West) and Barbara Brown (vice chairman, North Yorkshire East) to whom our thanks are due.

Chapter One

The Basics

COOKERY TERMS

Au gratin	Describes a dish which is coated in sauce, sprinkled with cheese or crumbs and browned in the oven or under the grill.
Blanching	Put food into saucepan, cover with cold water and bring to the boil, remove and plunge into cold water at once. Vegetables can be placed in boiling water, brought back to the boil and then plunged into cold water.
Blending	Careful mixing together of a dry and a liquid substance.
Braising	To brown meats or vegetables in a small amount of fat and then to cook them slowly in a very small amount of liquid in a covered pan, either on top of the stove or in the oven.
Bouillon	A meat broth, not clarified, that is to say, not strained.
Bouquet garni	A mixture of herbs, usually comprised of parsley, thyme and bay leaf wrapped in muslin; used for flavouring sauces and stews.
Clarified fat	Fat heated, skimmed and strained, to be used for greasing tins etc.
Creaming	To beat together either with a spoon, hand or mixer, fat and sugar until smooth and light in texture.
Croutons	Tiny cubes of bread, fried until golden brown and crisp and used as garnish for soups and other dishes.
Caramel	Concentrated sugar syrup which is boiled until the mixture becomes thick and golden brown in colour.
Folding	A method of lightly combining beaten egg whites or whipped cream with another mixture so that the air cells are not broken down; this should be done with a downward cutting motion of the spoon rather than stirring.

Kneading	A method of pressing, folding and stretching a dough with the hands mainly applicable to yeast doughs and the making of bread.
Marinade	A mixture of oil, lemon juice, vinegar or wine with seasonings and herbs in which meat or fish may be soaked before cooking, both to make it more tender and to improve its flavour.
Poaching	Food simmered in liquid, in an open pan, usually with just enough liquid to cover the food.
Pressure cooking	The method of cooking by steam in a specially constructed pan, at very high temperatures, so that foods are cooked much more quickly. Very useful for the long processes such as making stock for soup, or the bottling of fruit or vegetables.
To puree	Reducing one or a combination of cooked foods to a smooth pulp by putting them through a sieve.
Panada	A cooked paste of fat and flour (a roux) to which a liquid is added making a very thick sauce. Often forming a base for soufflés, and choux pastry.
Roux	Melted fat combined with an equal amount of flour, cooked over a gentle heat; a base for sauces, soups and gravies.
Sauté	Cooking meat or vegetables in very hot fat over a high flame, browning the outside as quickly as possible.
Simmer	To cook in liquid which is just boiling — when the bubbles appear at sides of the pan.
Stewing	The process of cooking food slowly in enough liquid to cover in a closed pot until tender.

OVEN TEMPERATURE CHART

Electricity		Gas	
Celsius	Fahrenheit		
110	225	$\frac{1}{4}$	Very Slow
125	250	$\frac{1}{2}$	Very Slow
140	275	1	Slow
150	300	2	Slow
165	325	3	Moderate
180	350	4	Moderate
190	375	5	Moderately hot
200	400	6	Moderately hot
220	425	7	Hot
230	450	8	Hot
240	475	9	Very Hot

The above is a guide only. As cookers vary please refer to your own cooker handbook.

Always follow either the metric measures or the imperial ones, do not change from one to another in a single recipe.

Level spoon measures have been used unless otherwise stated.

Chapter Two

Soups

LENTIL AND BACON SOUP

1 (15ml) tablespoon oil
4 oz (100g) streaky bacon,
chopped
1 onion, chopped
1 stick celery, chopped
1 bouquet garni
1 (15ml) tablespoon
tomato puree
2½ pints (1.5 litres)
chicken stock
8 oz (225g) split lentils
½ pint (300ml) plain
yoghurt
Celery leaves to garnish
SERVES 6

Heat oil in a large pan and fry bacon until crisp. Remove from pan with a slotted spoon and reserve a few pieces for garnish. Cook onion and celery in pan until soft. Add bouquet garni, tomato puree, stock and lentils, cover and simmer for 1 hour. Remove bouquet garni. Puree the soup with bacon in blender. Season and reheat. Serve garnished with a swirl of yoghurt, reserved bacon and celery leaves.

CREAM OF LOVAGE SOUP

½ oz (15g) butter or
margarine
6 oz (175g) onion chopped
2 cloves of garlic chopped
12 oz (350g) courgettes
sliced
8 oz (225g) potatoes peeled
and sliced
1¼ pints (750ml) water
2 tablespoons (30g) bouillon
powder or stock cube
Handful of lovage leaves (or
celery leaves)
Salt and pepper
Small tin of evaporated milk
(or ¼ pint (150ml) single cream)
SERVES 6

Melt fat, soften onion and garlic for 3 minutes. Add courgettes and potatoes and stir in. Add water, stock powder and lovage. Season lightly. Bring to boil and simmer for 20 minutes. Pour in cream. Puree or liquidise until smooth. Check seasoning and reheat.

BROCCOLI AND STILTON SOUP

1 oz (25g) butter
1 medium onion
¾ lb (300g) broccoli
1 medium potato
1 pint (600ml) chicken stock
1 teaspoon (5ml) cumin seeds
½ pint (300ml) milk
4 oz (100g) rindless Stilton
Salt and pepper
SERVES 6-8

Melt butter, chop onions. Break broccoli into florets, discarding tough stems, keeping 1 for garnish. Peel potato and add to pan with chicken stock and cumin seeds. Simmer for 20 minutes. Sieve or process and return to pan, add milk, but do not boil. Crumble in cheese, season and stir gently until cheese melts. Serve and garnish with broccoli.

SWEETCORN CHOWDER

4 oz (100g) streaky bacon
1 large onion
1 stick celery
1 large green pepper
2 medium potatoes
1 small bay leaf
¾ pint (450ml) water
Salt and pepper
1 oz (25g) flour or cornflour
1 pint (600ml) milk
2 cups sweetcorn kernels
Chopped parsley
SERVES 6

Chop the bacon, the onion and the celery stick. Blanch and chop the green pepper after removing the seeds. Dice the potatoes. Fry the chopped bacon in a deep pan until light brown. Add the chopped onion and celery and fry until coloured. Add the blanched pepper, diced potato, water and bay leaf and boil until the potato is cooked. Remove bay leaf. Blend flour (cornflour) with a little milk and then gradually add the rest of the pint. Add this to the contents of the pan and stir in the sweetcorn. Return to heat and bring to boil. Serve garnished with chopped parsley.

SHOOTING OR PICNIC SOUP

½ pint (300ml) milk
1 large tin baked beans
Touch of Worcester sauce or
curry powder
Tomato ketchup
Little chicken or game stock if
available
SERVES 4

Put milk into liquidiser. Add baked beans and liquidise until smooth. Transfer to a saucepan and add Worcester sauce or curry powder and tomato ketchup. Thin with stock if required. Heat, but do not boil. Transfer to thermos flask.

PLUM SOUP

1 lb (450g) plums
(damson/dark red plums)
Pinch of cinnamon
1 pint (600ml) water
To each pint of sieved soup
(600ml)
½ oz (12g) cornflour or
arrowroot
3-4 oz (75-100g) sugar
¼ pint (150ml) red wine
Whipped cream
SERVES 4-6

Halve and stone the plums. Tie the stones in a muslin bag. Put the plums, muslin bag, cinnamon and water into a pan and simmer gently until plums are soft. Rub fruit through a nylon sieve. Blend the cornflour with a little wine or water and stir into the soup. Reboil and stir the soup until it thickens. Sweeten. Add the remaining wine if used and then remove from the heat and allow to cool. Chill in individual serving dishes in the refrigerator. Whipped cream may be served separately or a swirl put on top of the soup.

LETTUCE SOUP

1 large onion
1 oz (25g) butter
12 oz (350g) large lettuce
½ oz (12g) flour
1 pint (600ml) chicken stock
Salt
Black pepper
SERVES 4

Slice onion and cook in butter for a few minutes. Shred the lettuce and add to the pan, cover and cook for a further 5 minutes. Stir in flour and gradually pour on the chicken stock and milk. Stir until the soup comes to the boil, cover and simmer gently for 20 minutes. Season. Liquidise in a blender, re-heat, then serve.

MUSHROOM SOUP

1 oz (25g) butter or margarine
1 oz (25g) plain flour
½ pint (300ml) chicken stock (1 cube)
½ pint (300ml) milk
4 oz (100g) mushrooms, finely chopped
Salt and pepper
1 tablespoon (15ml) lemon juice
2 tablespoons (30ml) fresh single cream
1 tablespoon (15ml) parsley
SERVES 3-4

Place all ingredients except lemon juice and cream into large saucepan. Whisking continuously over moderate heat, bring to boil, cover and simmer for 10 minutes. Remove from heat, add lemon juice and cream. Stir well and serve at once. Garnish with parsley.

CELERY SOUP

1 large head of celery
1 pint (600ml) milk
1 large potato
1 oz (25g) butter
1 pint (600ml) chicken stock
Large pinch grated nutmeg
Salt and pepper to taste
SERVES 6

Wash celery and chop finely, including leaves. Peel and finely dice the potato. Sauté the vegetables in the melted butter for 5 minutes. Add the stock, bring to the boil and then simmer for 30 minutes, until the vegetables are soft. Liquidise, or rub through a sieve. Return to pan and add milk, nutmeg and seasoning to taste. Heat through. Garnish with chopped parsley or grated cheese and serve with crusty bread.

HOT BORSCH

1 large carrot
2 medium onions
4 medium cooked beetroots
¼ pint (150ml) water
4 oz (125g) white cabbage
1 tablespoon lemon juice
Seasoning
4 tablespoons sour cream
SERVES 4

Finely grate onions, carrot and beetroots. Bring to the boil in ¼ pint water. Simmer for 30 minutes. Add stock, cabbage (shredded) and lemon juice. Season to taste and simmer for a further 20 minutes. Serve with a little sour cream poured over each portion.

WATERCRESS SOUP

2 bunches watercress
1 medium sized onion
1 medium sized potato
1 oz (25g) butter
¾ pint (450ml) milk
½ pint (300ml) chicken stock
Salt and pepper to taste
4 tablespoons fresh double cream
SERVES 4

Shred watercress (reserving some for garnish). Thinly dice onion and potato. Fry all in butter for 5 minutes (do not brown). Add milk and stock. Bring to boil. Cover and simmer gently for 10-15 minutes. Liquidise, or rub through a sieve. Season and reheat. When serving, whirl on cream and garnish.

LETTUCE SOUP

Follow recipe and method for Watercress Soup, using 1 large lettuce (shredded) instead.

CREAMY CARROT SOUP

8 oz (225g) carrots
1 large potato
1 medium sized onion
1 oz (25g) butter
¾ pint (450ml) water
¼ pint (150ml) milk
1 oz (25g) washed rice
1 level teaspoon salt and
pinch of grated nutmeg
2 teaspoons lemon juice
2 tablespoons fresh single
cream
SERVES 4

Gently fry grated carrot, potato and onion in butter for 5 minutes. Do not brown. Add water, milk, rice, nutmeg and salt. Bring to the boil, then simmer for 1 hour. Stir in lemon juice and cream.

CREAM OF POTATO SOUP

1 lb (450g) potatoes
1 large onion
2 celery stalks
1½ oz (40g) butter
¾ pint (450ml) water
1 level teaspoon salt and
shake of pepper
1 oz (25g) cornflour
2-3 tablespoons fresh
double cream
2 level tablespoons finely
chopped parsley
SERVES 4

Dice potatoes, thinly slice onion and celery and fry gently in butter for 10 minutes. Add water and seasoning. Bring to the boil. Cover pan and simmer very gently for 45 minutes. Liquidise (or sieve). Mix cornflour to smooth paste with a little of the milk. Stir in remainder. Bring to boil, stirring all the time, then simmer for 5 minutes. When serving, whirl cream on top and sprinkle with parsley.

ICED CUCUMBER AND YOGHURT

1 large unpeeled cucumber
½ small green pepper
(discarding pips)
2x5 oz (150g) cartons
natural yoghurt
2 tablespoons wine vinegar
2 tablespoons snipped chives
½ pint (300ml) chilled
milk
Seasoning to taste
SERVES 4-6

Grate cucumber and pepper. Mix in the vinegar and chives. Season and chill very thoroughly. Add chilled milk and yoghurt when ready to serve. Stir well. This is uncooked.

TOMATO AND ORANGE SOUP

1 large onion
1 oz (25g) butter
1 large tin tomatoes
2 teaspoons tomato puree
5 fl oz (150ml) stock
1 pint (600ml) milk
Grated rind 1 orange
6 peppercorns,
1 bay leaf
Pinch rosemary
SERVES 6

Peel and slice onion and cook in butter until transparent. Stir in tomatoes, stock, puree and flavourings. Bring to boil and simmer for 40 minutes. Remove flavourings and liquidise soup. Stir in grated orange rind and milk. Reheat, but do not boil. This soup is delicious served hot with grated cheese on top, or ice cold without cheese.

Chapter Three

Starters

AVOCADO STARTERS

2 medium sized avocados
A little lemon juice
SERVES 4

Fillings
CHEESE AND CELERY
8 oz (225g) cream cheese
2 tablespoons single cream
1 level teaspoon celery salt
1 teaspoon icing sugar
6 teaspoons lemon juice or
vinegar

Cut avocados in half 5 minutes before serving. Remove stones and brush with lemon juice to prevent browning. Fill cavities with one of the well mixed, chilled fillings. Garnish and serve in individual dishes.

YOGHURT
5 oz (150g) natural
yoghurt
2 tablespoons single cream
1 level teaspoon lemon
juice
1 level teaspoon icing sugar
½ level teaspoon salt

Note: Optional additions can be half a crushed clove of garlic, a little Worcester sauce, 1 level teaspoon paprika, 1 pinch cayenne pepper.

PRAWN
3 oz (90g) prawns
4 tablespoons mayonnaise
2 teaspoons single cream
1 teaspoon tomato ketchup
1 teaspoon finely chopped
green pepper
1 tablespoon chopped
parsley

TUNA COCKTAIL

7 oz (198g) tin tuna fish
1 tablespoon lemon juice
1 grapefruit
5 fl oz (150ml)
mayonnaise
Paprika pepper
Few lettuce leaves
SERVES 6

Chop tuna and mix with its oil and lemon juice. Peel grapefruit thickly, removing all pith. Cut flesh into segments and add to tuna mixture with mayonnaise. Mix well. Shred lettuce and put a little in each of six glasses. Pile tuna mixture on top and serve sprinkled with paprika.

GRAPEFRUIT AND ORANGE COCKTAIL

2 grapefruits
2 oranges
2 tablespoons (30ml)
caster sugar
Finely chopped mint
1 fl oz (28ml) light rum
SERVES 4

Halve grapefruit making serrated edges. Remove flesh in segments, cut oranges into segments. Combine orange and grapefruit segments and add the sugar and rum. Place mixture into grapefruit shells. Garnish with chopped mint and chill.

SMOKED HADDOCK ROULADE

8 oz (225g) uncoloured
smoked haddock
Milk
1½ oz (37g) butter
1 teaspoon (5ml) curry
powder
2½ tablespoons (37ml)
plain flour
¾ pint (450ml) milk
2-3 hard boiled eggs
4 eggs
1 oz (25g) grated cheese
SERVES 6

Cover haddock with milk and poach for 10 minutes. Cool and flake. Melt butter in pan with curry powder and cook gently for a minute. Add flour stirring well, then gradually add milk (use up milk from haddock to make up amount). Add 3-4 tablespoons (45-60ml) sauce. Add finely chopped eggs to sauce. Separate eggs, add yolks to fish with cheese and fold in beaten egg whites to sauce. Grease a 8x12 inch Swiss roll tin, line with non stick paper and grease again. Pour in mixture and level. Bake 10 minutes Gas Mark 6, 410F, 210C. or until risen and firm. Prepare a sheet of paper and sprinkle with cheddar cheese. Turn out cooked sauce onto cheese and spread fish mixture over, roll up and serve, seam side down, in slices.

FILO PARCELS WITH SAUCE ESPAGNOLE

2 sheets filo pastry
2 oz (50g) melted butter

Fillings
4 oz (100g) sautéd
mushrooms

4 oz (100g) spinach and
chopped hazelnuts

4 oz (100g) goats cheese

4 oz (100g) creamed
prawns

Sauce
2 oz (50g) butter
1 tablespoon (15ml)
chopped carrots
1 tablespoon (15ml)
chopped onion
1 tablespoon (15ml)
chopped celery
1 tablespoon (15ml)
chopped mushrooms
1 tablespoon (15ml) plain
flour
1 tablespoon (15ml)
tomato puree
½ pint (300ml) chicken
stock

Brush two sheets of filo with melted butter and place one on top of the other. Cut into six equal squares. Put a teaspoon (5ml) of one of the fillings in the centre of each square. Bring sides up together (like a Dorothy bag). Brush well with butter and arrange on baking tray. Cook for 10 minutes Gas Mark 4, 350F, 180. Arrange on plate flooded with sauce espagnole and garnish with parsley.

Soften all the vegetables in a pan with the butter. Add tomato puree and cook for a few minutes and add stock. Simmer for 20 minutes then sieve. Reheat to serve. Serves 2, double up for 4 servings.

BUTTERCUP MOULD

1 pint (600ml) aspic jelly
3 hard boiled eggs sliced
½ a cucumber peeled and
diced
3 medium celery sticks
diced
2 eating apples peeled, cored
and diced
1 medium tin pilchards
Juice of half lemon
Mayonnaise or salad cream

Alternative
2 tablespoons diced carrots
2 tablespoons sweetcorn
2 tablespoons diced potato
Mayonnaise or salad cream
SERVES 4-6

Make up the aspic jelly according to the instructions on the packet. Lightly oil or rinse with water a 1½ pint (75ml) ring mould, then overlap egg slices round the base. Cover with a little aspic jelly and refrigerate until set. Chill the rest of the aspic jelly until it is just beginning to thicken and set. Stir in the cucumber, celery and apples. Alternatively stir in the cooked vegetables, peas, carrots, sweetcorn and diced potatoes. Spoon into mould then chill until firm and set. Dip mould for a few seconds into very hot water, then turn out onto a plate. Fill the centre with mashed pilchards mixed with lemon juice and mayonnaise or salad cream. Alternatively fill the centre with diced cooked carrots, potatoes, peas and sweetcorn, mixed with mayonnaise or salad cream.

STUFFED COURGETTES

6 large courgettes
Salt and pepper
1 tablespoon (15ml)
sunflower oil
1 clove garlic
1 small onion
2 oz (50g) mushrooms
2 oz (50g) cream cheese
2 oz (50g) white
breadcrumbs
4-5 basil leaves or parsley,
finely chopped
1 oz (25g) Cheddar cheese,
grated
SERVES 6

Wash, trim and cut courgettes in half lengthways and place in boiling water for 4-5 minutes. Cool and drain on kitchen paper immediately. Scoop out centres and reserve pulp. Dry inside of shells and sprinkle with salt and pepper. Heat oil, add finely chopped garlic and onion, cook until soft. Add mushrooms and cook for a minute and cool slightly. Add chopped courgette pulp, cream cheese, crumbs, herbs and seasoning and mix well. Spoon filling into courgette shells and place in oiled shallow dish. Sprinkle with cheese and bake for 20-25 minutes, Gas Mark 6, 400F, 200C, until golden.

PRAWN AND AVOCADO RAMEKINS

8 oz (225g) peeled prawns
1 large avocado
1 oz (25g) ready salted
crisps
Sauce
1 oz (25g) butter
1 oz (25g) plain flour
½ pint (300ml) milk
4 oz (100g) grated cheese
Salt and ground black
pepper
SERVES 6

Place sauce ingredients in saucepan except the cheese, using a wire whisk continuously, cook until ready then add 3 oz cheese. Preheat grill to high. Divide prawns between 6 ramekins or small heatproof dishes. Peel and slice avocado and mix with the prawns. Spoon over enough sauce to cover. Sprinkle with crushed crisps and remaining cheese. Grill until bubbling. Garnish with slices of lemon and sprigs of parsley. Serve hot with brown bread and butter.

FISHERMAN'S COTTAGE

Filling
3 tablespoons (45ml) cream
4 oz (125g) cottage cheese
with pineapple
1 stick chopped celery
½ small red pepper
5 oz (125g) prawns
Squeeze lemon juice

Chopped fennel and
cucumber
Cayenne or paprika pepper
Mixed chopped salad
SERVES 2

Blend cream with cheese and stir in filling ingredients. Chill. Put 1 tablespoon (15ml) chopped salad in tall glasses then add 2 tablespoons (30ml) filling, finish with 1 tablespoon (15ml) salad. Garnish with slice of lemon, cayenne or paprika and a large prawn.

SOLE ROULADE

8 oz (225g) spinach
2 oz (50g) butter
4 fillets of lemon sole
Seasoning
2 oz (50g) smoked salmon
N.B. as an alternative to
smoked salmon. 2 oz (50g)
peeled shrimps or prawns
may be used.
SERVES 4

Blanch the spinach in boiling salted water for a few minutes. Melt the butter. Prepare 4 strips of metal foil wide enough and long enough to wrap the fillets. Shiny side uppermost brush the foil with a coating of melted butter. Place each well flattened fillet of lemon sole on the foil. Brush with butter. Season. Cover with a thin layer of smoked salmon, brush with butter, then cover the salmon with a layer of spinach. Brush with butter. Roll up the fillet tightly enclosing in the foil to make a firm roulade. Screw up the ends very tightly. Place on a baking sheet in a preheated oven. Cooking time: 25 minutes. Oven temperatures Gas Mark 4, 350F, 180C. Unwrap carefully and serve immediately.

CRAB STUFFED MUSHROOMS

8 large mushrooms
1 oz (25g) butter
1 small onion
2 tablespoons (25g) plain
flour
¼ pint (150ml) single cream
2 teaspoons lemon juice
1 tablespoon (15ml) sherry
Salt and pepper
7 oz (200g) tin white crab
meat
Topping
2 oz (50g) Gruyere cheese,
grated
1 tablespoon (15ml) fresh
breadcrumbs
Paprika
SERVES 4

Remove stems from mushrooms. Place in buttered shallow ovenproof dish, in a single layer. Melt butter and soften finely chopped onion, stir in flour, add cream, lemon juice, sherry (optional), salt and pepper and bring to the boil. Remove from heat and stir in drained crab meat.

Filling: Fill mushroom cavities with the mixture. Top with cheese and crumbs combined together. Sprinkle with paprika pepper and bake for 15 minutes at Gas Mark 6, 400F, 200C. May be served as a starter or main meal.

SAVOURY STUFFED PEARS

4 oz (100g) cottage cheese
4 oz (100g) cream cheese
Juice of ½ lemon
Salt and pepper
1 oz (25g) chopped
walnuts
Cucumber, small amount,
chopped
1 oz (25g) prawns
3 pears
Paprika
Lettuce to garnish
Tomato, to garnish
SERVES 6

Mix cheeses together with half a teaspoon of lemon juice, salt and pepper. Divide filling into two. Add chopped walnuts and cucumber to one half and prawns to the other. Prepare the pears; peel, cut in half and core. Brush with lemon juice. Add filling, 3 with prawns and 3 with cucumber and walnut. Sprinkle with paprika. Arrange on serving dish garnished with lettuce or tomato.

SMOKED MACKEREL PÂTÉ

6 oz (175g) block
margarine
8 oz (225g) smoked
mackerel
4 oz (100g) cottage cheese
5 fl oz (150ml) natural
yoghurt
1½ (22ml) tablespoons
lemon juice
Pinch of nutmeg
Pinch of cayenne pepper
Lemon slices, to garnish
Parsley, to garnish
SERVES 10

Melt margarine and pour into liquidiser. Add all other ingredients and liquidise until smooth. Pour into suitable dish if using as a starter or into smaller containers if freezing the pâté. Garnish with lemon slices and parsley. Serve as a starter.

AVOCADO DIP (GUACAMOLE)

2 large avocado pears
3 large tomatoes
1 small onion
¼ pint (150ml) soured
cream
1 tablespoon (15ml) lemon
juice
3 tablespoons (45ml)
mayonnaise
Salt and pepper

Halve the avocado pears, discard stone, remove the flesh and mash together. Chop remaining ingredients very finely and add to avocado mix (with a little Tabasco sauce if preferred). Serve with crisps, raw vegetables and crispbreads.

BACON STUFFED COURGETTES

4 medium courgettes
½ oz (12g) butter
1 medium onion
½ lb (225g) streaky bacon
2 tomatoes, peeled and
chopped
¼ teaspoon mixed herbs
Salt and pepper
SERVES 4

Wipe courgettes and slice off a thin wedge lengthwise. Scoop out the flesh. Finely chop the onion and courgette. Chop or mince the bacon. Melt the butter and fry the onion for 5 minutes. Add the bacon and chopped courgette and fry for a further 10 minutes. Skin and chop the tomatoes. Add these with herbs and seasonings. Mix well and pile into courgettes. Bake in greased ovenproof dish covered with foil for about 40 minutes at Gas mark 4, 350F, 180C. Serve on individual oval dishes, garnished with parsley and tomato.

EGGS EN COCOTTE

1 packet frozen spinach
Juice of ½ lemon
Pinch of black pepper
6 eggs
4 oz (125g) ham (lean)
6 tablespoons single cream
Pinch of dry mustard
SERVES 6

Divide spinach (small packet) between 6 greased ramekins. Sprinkle with lemon juice and black pepper. Break an egg into each ramekin. Mince or chop the ham finely. Sprinkle on top of the eggs and add cream. Sprinkle with mustard, and bake for 25 minutes at Gas Mark 4, 350F, 180C. Serve at once, garnished with a little fresh parsley.

STUFFED PEACHES

4 large peach halves
12 oz (350g) cottage
cheese
5 tablespoons mayonnaise
or soured cream
4 oz (125g) salted cashew
nuts
Freshly ground black pepper
Lettuce to garnish, black
grapes/or olives
SERVES 4

Mix mayonnaise with cottage cheese, nuts and pepper. Drain peach halves very well and place on crisp lettuce leaves on individual plates. Pile cheese mixture into each peach and top with a black olive or grape. Chill before serving.

SAVOURY MEAT LOAF
(A type of country pâté)

1 oz (25g) butter
1 large onion
1 fresh red pepper
1 lb (450g) sausage meat
or finely minced pork
8 oz (225g) fresh
breadcrumbs
1 cooking apple
2 tablespoons chopped fresh
parsley
1 teaspoon chopped sage
Grated rind of ½ lemon
Seasoning
1 egg
Watercress and red pepper,
to garnish.
SERVES 8

Melt the butter and fry finely chopped onions until soft. De-seed the red pepper. Reserve 8 thin strips and chop the rest. Peel and grate the apple. Mix meat, onion, pepper, apple, breadcrumbs, herbs, seasoning, lemon rind with well beaten egg. Grease a loaf tin and press in the mixture. Smooth the top and cover with foil. Bake until firm to the touch (about 1 hour 30 minutes at Gas Mark 5, 375F, 190C in the centre of the oven). Serve when cold, cut into slices and garnished with strips of red pepper and watercress.

PINEAPPLE TOPPERS

4 thick slices of wholemeal
bread
2 oz (50gm) butter or
peanut butter
4 oz (125gm) cottage
cheese or cream cheese
1 tablespoon chopped chives
or spring onion
4 large crisp lettuce leaves
4 pineapple rings
4 ripe cherries to garnish
SERVES 4

Cut slices of bread into rounds with large pastry cutter or kitchen scissors. Spread generously with butter or peanut butter. Blend cheese with finely chopped chives or spring onions. Cover buttered bread with crisp lettuce leaves and top with cheese mixture. Put ring of pineapple (well drained) on top of cheese and top with a fresh cherry. Serve on individual plates.

TUNA BAKES

7 oz (198g) tin tuna fish
10 oz (275g) tin
condensed mushroom soup
1 oz (25g) fresh white
breadcrumbs
2 oz (50g) butter
A few button mushrooms
4 sprigs of parsley
SERVES 4

Drain fish and flake. Heat soup in a small pan. Add fish and cook gently for 3 minutes. Divide mixture between 4 greased scallop shells. Sprinkle each with breadcrumbs and dot with half the butter. Grill until golden brown. Wash and dry the mushrooms. Melt remaining butter, add mushrooms and cook gently for 5 minutes. A little crushed garlic can be added to the melted butter if desired. Use mushrooms and parsley to garnish each shell before serving.

WALDORF SALADS (INDIVIDUAL)

4 medium eating apples
1 stick of celery
1 oz (25g) chopped
walnuts
5 fl oz (150ml)
mayonnaise
SERVES 4

Remove tops from apples. Core carefully and then scoop out inside of the apple. Chop this into small pieces and mix at once with mayonnaise. Scrub and grate the celery. Add this, with chopped nuts, to the apple mixture. Season. Pack into apple shells and replace tops. Serve on a crisp lettuce leaf on individual plates.

TUNA TOMATOES

4 beef tomatoes
Salt
2x7 oz (2x200g) cans of
tuna in brine, drained
3 oz (85g) fromage frais
1 teaspoon (5ml) tomato
puree, or ketchup
Finely grated rind and
juice of 1 lemon
½ red pepper, ½ yellow
pepper, deseeded and
chopped
Pepper to season
Strips of lemon peel, to
garnish
SERVES 4

Cut a slice from the top of each tomato. Remove seeds and sprinkle the inside with a little salt. Flake the tuna and stir in all the other ingredients. Mix together and season. Divide between the tomatoes and garnish with lemon peel. Chill until required. This may be served on lettuce or watercress leaves for a starter. If served as a main course, serve with a salad.

Salmon or any other canned fish may be used instead of tuna. Alternatively this mixture may be placed on raw mushrooms instead of tomatoes.

PRAWN STUFFED EGGS

6 hard boiled eggs
1 slice of onion
6 peppercorns
1 tablespoon of flour
Pepper
Salt
4 oz (100g) prawns
¼ pint (150ml) milk
Blade mace
3½ oz (90g) butter
3 oz (75g) cream cheese
Watercress, to garnish

(Prawns can be substituted with cooked chopped ham or chicken, or sliced cooked mushrooms.)

Heat milk with onion, mace and peppercorns. Cover and leave to infuse. Put ½ oz butter in a pan, heat gently and blend in flour. Gradually add the infused milk, season to taste. Stirring continuously, bring to the boil, cook for 1 minute. Turn on to a plate, cover with cling film to prevent a skin forming and leave sauce until cold. Cream remaining butter until soft. Split hard-boiled eggs in two, scoop out the yolks and rub through a sieve. Keep the whites in a bowl of water. Work the yolks with the butter, cheese and cold sauce. Chop half the prawns finely, add to the mixture and season to taste. Drain and dry the egg whites, put filling into a piping bag with a plain nozzle and fill egg whites. Scatter over the remaining prawns, dust with paprika, place on a dish with watercress in the centre.

Chapter Four

Fish

COD WITH MUSHROOMS

1 lb (450g) cod fillet
Salt and pepper
1 tomato, skinned and
sliced
2 oz (50g) mushrooms,
chopped
1 small bottle cider
¾ oz (18g) margarine
½ oz (12g) flour
Creamed potatoes
A little grated cheese
1 sliced tomato, skinned
Parsley, to garnish
SERVES 4

Cut the cod into small pieces and put into a fireproof dish with a little salt and pepper, the sliced and skinned tomato and the chopped mushrooms. Almost cover the fish with the cider and dot the top with the margarine. Cover with foil and bake in a moderate hot oven Gas Mark 5, 375F, 190C for about 30 minutes. Strain off the liquid and use to make a sauce with the rest of the margarine and flour, season to taste and pour it over the fish. Pipe creamed potato round the edge of the dish. Sprinkle the fish with the grated cheese, garnish with slices of tomato, return to oven for 10-15 minutes to brown. Decorate with the parsley and serve with a green vegetable.

FISH WITH PAPRIKA RICE

1 lb (450g) cod fillet
Lemon juice
Salt and pepper
1 pint (600ml) chicken
stock
8 oz (225g) long grain
rice
1 tablespoon (15ml)
paprika pepper
8 oz (225g) tin of
tomatoes
SERVES 4

Cut fish into pieces, sprinkle with lemon juice and salt. Pour the stock into a saucepan and bring to the boil. Add fish, rice, paprika and pepper. Drain tomatoes and stir the liquid into the rice. Bring back to boil, stir once, cover and simmer for 15 minutes or until the rice and fish are tender and the liquid is absorbed. Chop tomatoes roughly and stir into rice mixture and reheat. Serve with a tossed green salad.

FISHERMAN'S TART

Pastry
8 oz (225g) plain flour
4 oz (100g) butter or
margarine
2 oz (50g) lard
1 size 2 egg (beaten)
1 tablespoon cold water
Filling
10 oz (275g) smoked cod
2 tablespoons (30ml) oil
(olive or sunflower)
2 oz (50g) peeled prawns
1 large avocado
1 teaspoon (5ml) ground
mace
1 clove garlic
½ pint (300ml) double
cream
1 size 3 egg
Juice of ½ lemon
Salt and pepper
SERVES 8-10

For the pastry sift flour with a pinch of salt into a bowl. Put the fats into the flour and rub in lightly until crumb-like. Mix in the beaten egg and cold water with a knife. Gather gently into a ball and roll out in a circle. Butter a 10-11 inch shallow flan dish and line with the pastry. Refrigerate for at least 30 minutes. Heat the oven Gas Mark 6, 400F, 200C and bake blind for 20-25 minutes. Leave to cool.

For the filling cut the fish into 1 inch cubes, heat oil in a frying pan and stir the fish over a gentle heat for 5-8 minutes. Transfer to a mixing bowl and add prawns (reserving 3 for decoration). Cut the avocado in half, peel and cut into slices. Add to the mixture, stir in the mace and garlic. Whip cream until beginning to thicken, add the egg, lemon juice and seasoning and continue whipping until thick. Stir in the cooled fish mixture. Pour into pastry case. Cook in the centre of the oven, temperature Gas Mark 5, 375F, 190C for 15-20 minutes. Cool and decorate with the prawns. The tart should be served cold but do not refrigerate. Suitable for picnics or as a starter.

SHRIMP CHEESE DELIGHT

8 oz (225g) prepared shrimps
10 oz tin of condensed
cream of mushroom soup
6 oz (175g) cooked rice
3 oz (75g) grated cheese
A little tomato ketchup
Chopped parsley for garnish
SERVES 3-4

Mix the shrimps, soup, cheese, rice and a little ketchup. Place in an ovenproof dish and bake in the centre of a moderate oven (Gas Mark 4, 350F, 180C) for 30 minutes. Pile on to a hot dish and garnish with parsley.

FISH CAKES

10 oz (275g) old potatoes
12 oz (350g) white fish
fillet
1 ½ oz (40g) butter
Salt and pepper
1 tablespoon (15ml)
freshly chopped parsley
1 teaspoon (5ml) lemon
juice
1 small egg
2 small packets potato
crisps
6 tablespoons (90ml) oil
MAKES 6-8 CAKES

Peel potatoes and boil in lightly salted water until tender, then drain very thoroughly. Mash in the saucepan. Meanwhile put another saucepan of water to boil and cut the fish fillet into several pieces. Use a little of the butter to grease a plate and a piece of greaseproof paper to cover the fish. Lay the fish on buttered plate, season with salt and pepper and cover with the buttered greaseproof paper. Set the plate over the saucepan of boiling water, cover with the lid and steam for 10 minutes. Drain off the liquid, remove any skin and bones and flake the fish. Beat the remaining butter into the mashed potato and add fish and parsley. Add the lemon juice and seasoning to taste, beat until smoothly mixed. Turn onto a plate cover loosely and leave until cold and firm. Divide the cooled mixture into 6 or 8 portions and on a lightly floured surface shape the portions into ovals. Beat the egg. Tip the potato crisps into a strong plastic bag and crush finely with a rolling pin. Dip fish cakes in egg. Turn the crushed crisps onto a piece of greaseproof paper and coat each fish cake thoroughly. Use a palette knife to press the crumbs on and re-shape the cakes. Heat the oil in a large frying pan over medium heat. When very hot fry a single layer of cakes until golden then turn carefully and brown other side. Lift out with fish slice, draining briefly over pan, then thoroughly on crumpled kitchen paper. Keep hot while frying the remaining cakes and serve immediately.

CREAMY FINNAN PANCAKES

½ pint (300ml) pancake
batter
4 tablespoons (60ml)
clarified butter or oil
½ lb (225g) boil in the
bag smoked haddock
2 oz (50g) cheddar cheese
1 small onion
1 stick celery
2 oz (50g) mushrooms
2 oz (50g) butter
¼ pint (150ml) thick
cream
Freshly ground black pepper
1 tablespoon (15ml)
chopped chives
SERVES 4

Start cooking the haddock following manufacturers instructions. Grate the cheese while the haddock is cooking, make the batter. Make 12 pancakes greasing the pan with the clarified butter or oil. Keep the pancakes hot on a plate over a pan of hot water. Place kitchen paper between each layer and cover the pile with foil. Peel and finely chop the onion. Scrub and chop the celery stick, wipe and thinly slice the mushrooms. Place 1 oz (25g) butter in a frying pan over medium heat and gently fry the onion, celery and mushrooms for 4 minutes. Drain. Remove the haddock from the bag and drain. Flake and stir in the fried vegetables. Stir the cream into the mixture. Season to taste with freshly ground black pepper and stir in the chopped chives. Butter a shallow flame proof dish with the remaining butter. Place 2 tablespoons of the fish mixture on one edge of the pancakes and roll up. Place in dish. Stuff others in the same way and arrange slightly overlapping in the dish. Set the grill to its highest heat. Sprinkle the cheese over the pancakes, place under grill for 3 minutes until the cheese is golden and bubbling.

SALMON FLAN

8 inch pastry case
8 oz (225g) tin salmon
6 oz (175g) cottage cheese
with fresh chives
2 eggs; 1 egg yolk
Four drops of lemon juice
Salt and pepper
¼ pint (150ml) single cream

Flake fish and remove bones. Mix all ingredients together and add fresh chives if possible with plain cottage cheese or use the cottage cheese already combined with chives. Spoon the mixture into the uncooked shortcrust pastry case and bake at Gas Mark 6, 400F, 200C. for 30 minutes or until firm.

FAMILY FISH PIE

1 lb (450g) cod, haddock,
coley etc.
4 oz (125g) cooked frozen
peas
1 oz (25g) plain flour
1 oz (25g) margarine plus
½ oz (15g)
½ pint (300ml) milk plus
2 tablespoons
Seasoning
2 hard boiled eggs, chopped
2 tablespoons (30ml)
mayonnaise
1 lb (450g) potatoes
Parsley and tomatoes, to
garnish
1½ pint (900ml) dish
SERVES 4

Peel and cut potatoes into even sized pieces. Place in a pan of boiling salted water. Wash and skin fish, place on a metal plate over potatoes and sprinkle with seasoning and 2 tablespoons milk. Cover with pan lid and steam for approx. 20 minutes. Melt margarine in a small pan, stir in flour and cook for 1 minute. Remove from heat and blend in half a pint of milk. Return to heat and cook until sauce thickens. Add peas, chopped hard boiled eggs, mayonnaise and seasoning. Flake fish and add to sauce, pour into dish. Mash potatoes adding ½ oz (15g) margarine and 2 tablespoons milk. Beat with a wooden spoon to achieve a creamy texture. Place into a piping bag fitted with a large star nozzle. Pipe potatoes over the top of the sauce in the dish and garnish.

EGG AND HADDOCK CRUMBLE

12 oz (350g) cooked
flaked smoked haddock
½ lb (225g) sliced and
cooked carrots
Juice ½ a lemon
Salt and pepper
5 hard boiled eggs
Lemon slices
1 oz (25g) butter
1 oz (25g) flour
½ pint (300ml) milk
4 oz (125g) brown
breadcrumbs
3 oz (75g) grated Cheddar
SERVES 4

Heat 1 oz (25g) butter in a saucepan, stir in 1 oz (25g) flour and cook for 1 minute. Remove from heat and gradually add half a pint (300ml) of milk. Bring to the boil, stirring until thickened. Remove from heat. Add 12 oz (350g) cooked flaked smoked haddock, ½ lb (225g) sliced and cooked carrots, lemon juice, salt and pepper. Roughly chop 4 hard boiled eggs and mix into the mixture. Turn into a medium ovenproof dish. Mix 4 oz (125g) brown breadcrumbs and 3 oz (75g) grated cheese together, season lightly, sprinkle over haddock. Bake at Gas Mark 6, 400F, 200C (preheated) for 30 minutes or until topping is golden. Cut another hard boiled egg into quarters. Garnish top with egg and lemon slices.

FISH PROVENÇAL

½ oz (15g) butter
1 small chopped onion
½ deseeded chopped green pepper
Seasoning
2 oz (50g) lean bacon
8 oz (250g) white fish fillet
8 oz (250g) tin tomatoes
1 bay leaf
SERVES 2

Melt ½ oz (15g) butter in a pan and fry 1 small chopped onion, a half of a deseeded and chopped green pepper and 2 oz (50g) derinded and chopped lean bacon until soft. Cut 8 oz (250g) skinned white fish fillet into cubes. Toss into 1 tablespoon (15ml) seasoned flour then fry with the vegetables for 2-3 minutes. Stir in a 8 oz (227g) can of tomatoes, 1 bay leaf and seasoning. Bring to the boil then cover and simmer for 10-15 minutes until fish is tender. Remove bay leaf and serve.

RUSSIAN FISH PIE

6 oz (165g) frozen flaky pastry
8 oz (225g) cod, coley, haddock or other white fish
Sauce
½ oz (15g) margarine
½ oz (15g) flour
¼ pint (125ml) milk
Seasoning
Parsley
Glaze, beaten egg
Garnish, parsley
SERVES 2-4

Steam fish between two plates over a pan of boiling water. Make coating sauce by roux method, season to taste. Chop parsley finely and stir into sauce. Roll out flaky pastry to 8-9 inch. (30-35 cm) square, trim off edges, lightly mark diagonals. Flake steamed fish (remove bones and skin) into parsley sauce, stir thoroughly. Place fish mixture into centre of pastry. Damp edges with a little of the glaze. Fold up edges into an envelope shape, seal well and flute using back of knife. Brush over with glaze. Make pastry leaves from pastry trimmings, decorate top of envelope, glaze leaves. Bake for about an hour at Gas Mark 7, 425F, 220C, reducing heat after the first 10 minutes to Gas Mark 5, 375F, 190C. Serve on an oval plate, garnished with parsley.

FILLETS OF PLAICE WITH CHEESE STUFFING

4 plaice fillets
5 dessertspoons
breadcrumbs
2 teaspoons chopped parsley
4 oz (125g) grated cheese
Grated lemon rind
Pepper and salt
1 egg
SERVES 4

Wash and dry fillets. Chop parsley. Mix breadcrumbs, parsley, salt, grated rind of half a lemon and grated cheese. Spread this mixture on to the fillets. Roll each into a sausage shape and secure with a cocktail stick or fine string. Put into well buttered dish into which they fit closely. Cover with foil and bake for about 20 minutes at Gas Mark 4, 350F, 180C. Serve with white sauce.

SALMON CREAM FLAN

Shortcrust Pastry
4 oz (125g) plain flour
1 oz (25g) lard
1 oz (25g) hard margarine
Salt
Filling
7½-8 oz (200g) tin of
salmon
2 eggs
¼ medium cucumber
½ pint (300ml) single
cream
¼ teaspoon anchovy essence
(optional)
½ small onion
Seasoning
Garnish
Thinly sliced cucumber
Parsley
SERVES 4

Make shortcrust pastry and line an 8 inch plain flan ring with pastry, then with greaseproof paper and fill with baking beans. Bake for 10-15 minutes at Gas Mark 5, 375F, 190C. Flake salmon into a basin, beat in eggs. Peel and dice cucumber. Finely chop or grate onion. Mix onion, cucumber, cream, anchovy essence and seasoning with salmon and eggs. Remove baking beans and paper. Turn mixture into pastry case. Lower oven and place flan in oven 30-35 minutes at Gas Mark 3, 325F, 170C until pastry is crisp and filling is firm. Garnish with thinly sliced cucumber arranged around the edge of the flan.

SALMON OR TUNA COULIBIAC

8 oz (200g) cod, coley or
haddock
6½ oz (185g) tin of tuna
or salmon
1 small onion
2 oz (50g) patna rice
Salt and pepper
2 oz (50g) mushrooms
½ oz (10g) margarine
1 hard boiled egg
½ teaspoon (2.5ml) lemon
juice
8 oz (200g) packet puff
pastry
Beaten egg or milk to glaze
Sprig of parsley to garnish
SERVES 4-6

Poach fish in ¼ pint (150ml) of water, drain and reserve liquid. Drain tuna or salmon and add liquid to fish liquor making up to ¼ pint (150ml) with water. Peel and chop onion, put in pan with rice, fish liquid and lightly season. Simmer until rice is tender and drain. Slice mushrooms and cook in margarine for 1-2 minutes. Mix together the rice, mushrooms, chopped hard boiled egg, drained fish, salmon or tuna and lemon juice and lightly season. Roll the pastry out to approximately 10 inch (25cm) square. Place pastry diagonally on lightly greased baking sheet with the corners hanging over the edges of the baking sheet; this makes the finished coulibiac square on the tin. Place filling in the centre of the pastry and form into a square, with sides parallel to the tin and not the pastry. Brush edges of pastry with egg or milk and bring corners to the centre to form a square over the filling. Seal edges by pinching together decoratively and brush over with egg or milk. Bake middle to top oven Gas Mark 7, 425F, 220C, for 15 minutes and then reduce to Gas Mark 5, 375F, 190C, for 20 minutes until well risen and golden. Garnish and serve hot with vegetables, parsley or tartare sauce.

CHICKEN OF THE SEA

1x7 oz (200g) tin tuna
4 oz (100g) mushrooms
Frozen vegetables
1 small tine of condensed
tomato soup, alternatively
mushroom soup.
SERVES 2-3

Place layers of tuna (drained), uncooked mushrooms and vegetables in an ovenproof dish and add soup. Cover with a lid and cook for 20-30 minutes at Gas Mark 5, 375F, 190C. Serve with boiled rice. This can be served as a light lunch dish.

BAKED SALMON STEAKS

4 salmon steaks about ½
inch thick
Butter
Salt and pepper
1 cucumber
Lemon slices
SERVES 4

Wash, dry and trim the salmon steaks. Butter a large piece of foil and use to line a roasting tin. Arrange the salmon steaks on the foil. Season with salt and pepper and top each with a knob of butter. Cover with a lid of foil and bake in the centre of a fairly hot oven (Gas Mark 6, 400F, 200C) for 20-25 minutes. Meanwhile peel and dice the cucumber. Heat 2oz (50g) butter and sauté the diced cucumber for 10-15 minutes, stir frequently and use only a gentle heat. Season the cucumber well. When the salmon is cooked arrange on a serving dish surrounded by the cucumber. Top with lemon slices and serve hollandaise sauce separately.

SOLE IN WHITE SAUCE

2 soles filleted
Salt and pepper
2 oz (50g) butter
About ½ pint (300ml) dry
white wine
½ oz (15g) flour
2 egg yolks
Shrimps and parsley to
garnish
SERVES 2

Wipe and season the fillets and roll up, arrange in a buttered ovenproof dish. Dot with 1 oz (25g) of the butter and pour ¼ pint (150ml) of the white wine over. Cover and bake in the centre of a moderate oven (Gas Mark 4, 350F, 180C) for 20 minutes. Arrange the fish on a warmed serving dish and keep warm. Measure the liquid and make up to half a pint with more wine. Make a white sauce with ½ oz (15g) butter, the flour and fish liquid. Cook for 2-3 minutes then remove from the heat and beat in the egg yolks and remaining butter. Season well and reheat but do not allow to boil. Pour over the fish. Serve garnished with shrimps and parsley.

CRISPY LEMON SOLE

4x8-10 oz (225-275g)
lemon sole, or plaice fillets
(skinned)
4 rashers back bacon
Salt and black pepper
Lemon juice
1 oz (25g) butter
2 oz (50g) grated cheddar
cheese
1x1oz (25g) packet of
potato crisps, slightly
crushed
SERVES 4

Place each fillet on top of a rasher of bacon. Season with salt and pepper and sprinkle with some lemon juice. Roll up the fillets from head to tail, and place in an ovenproof dish, ensuring that the tails are secured underneath. Dot with butter, and bake at Gas Mark 6, 400F, 200C for 15 minutes until golden brown. Remove the dish from the oven, sprinkle with cheese and crisps, return to oven for a further 14 minutes until golden brown. Serve garnished with tomato wedges, and fresh vegetables.

COD STEAKS WITH MUSTARD

4 cod steaks
2 tablespoons lemon juice
4 teaspoons made mustard
Knob of butter
Salt and pepper
SERVES 4

Place steaks in a lightly greased grill pan, season with lemon and dot with butter. Grill for 4 to 5 minutes. Turn once if necessary. Spread each steak with mustard, continue cooking for a further 2 minutes.

TASTY TUNA FISH DISH

8 oz (200g) tuna, drained
2 oz (50g) cooked noodles
1/2 an onion, finely chopped
1 tin condensed mushroom
soup
2 tablespoons sherry
2 oz (50g) grated Cheddar
cheese
SERVES 2-3

Put the soup, tuna, onion, noodles and sherry in an ovenproof dish, fold in half the cheese and mix all together. Sprinkle the remaining cheese on top, bake in the oven (Gas Mark 4, 350F, 180C) for 30-35 minutes.

STUFFED WHITING

6 medium sized whiting
1 large orange
1 small onion
2 slices wholemeal bread
2 tablespoons (30ml)
freshly chopped parsley
1 lemon
Salt
Freshly ground black pepper
2 oz (50g) butter
SERVES 6

Using a serrated knife, scrape the fish skin to dislodge loose scales. Cut off the fins using kitchen scissors. Make a slit along the underside of the fish. Pull out the innards working from tail to head. Rinse the inside of the fish under cold running water and pat dry with a kitchen towel. Peel orange and cut the segments free from the membrane keeping it on a plate or grooved board to avoid loss of juice. Chop roughly and place the juice and flesh in a bowl. Discard pips and pith. Peel and finely chop the onion. Add to the bowl. Reduce the bread to crumbs, chop the parsley. Squeeze the remaining juice from the orange membrane. Add these ingredients to the bowl. Season to taste then mix with a fork until well blended.

Make 2-3 diagonal cuts in the flesh along each side of the fish. Divide the stuffing equally between the fish putting it into the cavity where the innards were. Do not over stuff. Heat the grill to moderate. Melt the butter in a heavy based pan over low heat. Do not allow to brown. Sprinkle each fish on both sides with salt rubbing in the salt with your finger tips. Then brush with melted butter. Place the fish under the grill about 4 inches away from the heat. Grill for 10 minutes. Turn carefully with a fish slice and a round-bladed knife to avoid breaking. Then cook for a further 10 minutes on the second side.

CORN TUNA SKILLET

11 oz (275g) tin of whole
corn kernels
Tin tuna fish
2 eggs
1/4 pint (150ml) milk
Salt and pepper
1 packet onion sauce mix
2 oz (50g) Lancashire
cheese
SERVES 3-4

Grease a fairly shallow ovenproof dish holding one and three-quarter pints (1 litre) of liquid. Open the tins of corn and tuna fish and drain off the liquid. Tip the corn into the dish, then the tuna fish and break it up over the corn. Beat the eggs and milk together and season with salt and pepper; pour the mixture into the dish. Crumble the cheese, mix it with the dry onion sauce mix, and sprinkle them evenly over the mixture. Bake just above the centre of a moderate oven (Gas Mark 4, 350F, 180C) for about 25 minutes.

CURRIED TUNA AND PASTA BAKE

4 oz (100g) wholewheat
macaroni
1 oz (25g) butter
1 oz (25g) plain flour
1/4 pint (150ml) milk
Salt and pepper
7 oz (170g) tin tuna,
drained and flaked
8 oz (220g) tin sweetcorn,
drained
1 teaspoon curry powder
2 oz (50g) grated Cheddar
cheese
5 tablespoons yoghurt
1 oz (25g) freshly grated
Parmesan cheese
SERVES 2

Cook pasta in boiling salted water for 8-10 minutes. Meanwhile melt butter, add flour and cook for 2 minutes. Remove from heat and gradually stir in milk. Return to heat and stir until sauce thickens. Add tuna, sweetcorn, curry powder, cheese and yoghurt. Keep warm. Drain pasta, combine with sauce and divide between 2 individual ovenproof dishes. Sprinkle with freshly grated Parmesan and brown under grill. Serve immediately.

FISH IN A PIQUANT PARSLEY SAUCE

4 good sized fillets of white fish, folded over, end to end
Vegetable oil
Salt and ground white or black peppercorns
Sauce
8 oz (225g) carton of natural Greek yoghurt
4 teaspoons (20ml) Dijon mustard
4 teaspoons (20ml) lemon juice
1 tablespoon (15ml) chopped parsley or to taste
SERVES 4

Lightly grease a casserole dish with the vegetable oil, and bake the fish, seasoned with salt and pepper, and covered tightly, for 25 minutes at Gas Mark 5, 375F, 190C. Meanwhile, mix together the sauce ingredients. Pour over the cooked fish and serve immediately. Serve with jacket potatoes and a chunk of lemon and a green vegetable. A smaller quantity baked in individual dishes or ramekins makes a good starter.

LEMON STUFFED COD

4 cod steaks, skinned and bones removed
1 oz (25g) margarine or oil
4 oz (100g) mushrooms
1 small onion
Rind and juice of 1 lemon
1 teaspoon mixed herbs
2 wholemeal crispbreads, crushed, or 2 oz wholemeal breadcrumbs
3 tablespoons skimmed milk
Tomato wedges and parsley
Seasoning
SERVES 4

Place cod steaks in an ovenproof dish. Combine all ingredients for the stuffing, season and place in the centre of each cutlet. Pour in skimmed milk and cover with foil. Bake at Gas Mark 5, 375F, 190C for 20-25 minutes, and garnish with tomato and parsley. Alternatively use cod fillet and roll fillet around the stuffing.

FISH PIE

8 oz (200g) carrots
8 oz (200g) leeks
1 celery heart
1 lb (500g) potatoes
1 lb 8 oz (750g) white
fish, skinned and boned
¾ pint (450ml) skimmed
milk
4 tablespoons low fat
natural yoghurt
1 oz (25g)
polyunsaturated margarine
1 oz (25g) plain flour
2 teaspoons mustard
powder
Black pepper and ground
mace
1 lb (500g) tomatoes,
sliced
1 tablespoon chopped fish
herbs
SERVES 4

Put the potatoes to cook. Chop the carrots, leeks and celery and cook until tender. Poach the fish in skimmed milk for 10 minutes, drain and keep the liquid. Cut the fish into chunks. Melt the margarine, stir in the flour and cook for 1 minute. Stir in the milk from the fish and gradually cook until the sauce thickens and boils. Mix in the mustard and season with herbs, mace and pepper. Drain the vegetables. Mash the potatoes with yoghurt. Stir vegetables and fish into the sauce. Pour into an ovenproof dish, cover with sliced tomatoes and spread with mashed potato. Bake at Gas Mark 4, 350F, 180C for 15 minutes.

PLAICE AND ORANGE BAKE

4 fillets plaice (skinned)
1 oz (25g) margarine
Rind and juice of 1 orange
Parsley to garnish
Filling
1 small orange, peeled
1 small green pepper,
deseeded and halved
4 oz (100g) cottage cheese
Black pepper
SERVES 4

Cut both the orange and the pepper in half. Slice one half of each and reserve for garnishing. Chop the remaining orange and pepper. Mix with the cheese and black pepper. Divide the filling between the fillets and roll up. Place in an ovenproof dish and dot with margarine. Pour over the orange juice and sprinkle with the rind. Cover with foil and bake at Gas Mark 5, 375F, 190C for 40 minutes. Garnish with the orange and green pepper slices and parsley. Serve at once.

SALMON MOUSSE

7 oz (175g) tin red
salmon
Juice and finely grated rind
of half a lemon
1/4 oz (15g) powdered
gelatine
1/4 pint (150ml) double
cream
Seasoning
To serve
Cucumber, lemon wedges,
salad, brown bread and
butter.
SERVES 6

Drain the juice from the salmon into a basin. Sprinkle in the gelatine. Heat gently over a pan of hot water until completely dissolved. Allow to cool. Meanwhile flake the salmon, and whisk the cream until it is semi-thick. Blend all the ingredients with a fork or combine in a food processor for a few seconds (too much blending destroys the texture). Pour the mixture into a wetted mould and leave to set in a refrigerator. When ready to serve, turn out the mould onto a suitable dish, garnish with thinly sliced cucumber, lemon wedges and parsley. Serve accompanied by salad and brown bread and butter.

SAUCY FISH

1 lb (450g) white fish
4 oz (100g) prawns
(optional)
4 medium tomatoes, sliced
1 tin condensed asparagus
soup
Little lemon juice
Seasoning
Croutons to garnish
SERVES 4

Season the fish, sprinkle with lemon juice. Place on a plate, cover with cling film. Cook in the microwave oven on HIGH for 4 minutes or until the fish flakes easily with a fork. Empty the soup into a 2½ pint (1.5 litre) bowl, cover and heat in the microwave oven on medium for 3-4 minutes. stir in the flaked fish and prawns, season. Heat on high for 2 minutes then arrange the tomatoes attractively on top. Put in the microwave oven on high for 1 minute to heat the tomatoes. Garnish with the croutons and serve.

Instead of white fish, canned tuna fish may be substituted. Then a can of condensed chicken soup should be used, the prawns omitted and a little chopped onion added.

Chapter Five

Poultry

CHICKEN AND MUSHROOM COBBLER

1 oz (25g) butter
1 onion, chopped
4 oz (100g) button mushrooms
1 oz (25g) plain flour
½ pint (300ml) milk
Salt and pepper
1 lb (450g) cooked chicken cut into ¾ inch pieces
4 oz (100g) tinned or frozen sweetcorn
3 oz (75g) fresh or frozen peas
1 tablespoon (15ml) fresh parsley
Scone Topping
8 oz (225g) self raising flour
2 oz (50g) butter
¼ pint (150ml) milk
6 oz (175g) Cheddar cheese (finely grated and of mature flavour)
SERVES 4

Melt butter and fry onions and mushrooms. Add the flour and gradually mix in the milk. Gently bring to the boil. Stirring all the time. Season to taste. Add chicken, sweetcorn, peas and parsley. Place mixture in large ovenproof dish. For the scone topping, rub the butter into the flour and add milk to make a smooth dough. Roll out to a rectangle 8x12 inch. Sprinkle the dough with 5 oz of the grated cheese, then roll up like a Swiss roll. Cut the roll into slices approximately ¾ inch thick and arrange on top of the chicken, round the edge of the dish. Sprinkle with remaining cheese. Bake for 20 minutes at Gas Mark 7, 425F, 220C, then reduce the heat to Gas Mark 5, 375F, 190C for a further 20 minutes, until the cheese is nicely browned. Sprinkle with chopped parsley and serve with green vegetables.

CHICKEN BREASTS IN LIME AND GIN SAUCE

4 chicken breasts, boneless
Oil and butter for frying
Sauce
1 medium onion, chopped
finely
Grated rind of 2 limes
1 teaspoon (5ml) grainy
French mustard
4 tablespoons (4x15ml)
apricot jam
1 teaspoon (5ml) tomato
puree
2 teaspoons (2x5ml) wine
or cider vinegar
4 tablespoons (4x15ml)
gin
1 teaspoon (5ml)
cornflour, blended with
4 tablespoons (4x15ml)
water plus 1 teaspoon
(5ml) stock powder or half
a stock cube, chicken
Salt and pepper
To Finish
1 oz (25g) flaked almonds,
toasted.
SERVES 4

Heat oil and butter in small frying pan and brown chicken breasts. Drain and place in ovenproof dish. Add onion to pan (you may need a little more fat) and cook until soft. Add the rest of the ingredients (except nuts) and bring up to boil. Season. Pour over chicken and cook at Gas Mark 5, 375F, 190C for 15 minutes covered. Remove cover, baste and put back in oven uncovered for another 15 minutes. Decorate each breast with nuts. Will freeze.

TANDOORI CHICKEN

1 teaspoon chilli powder
2 teaspoons garam masala
1 teaspoon salt
1 teaspoon ginger powder
¾ teaspoon garlic powder
1 teaspoon mango powder
2 tablespoons (30ml) plain yoghurt
2 tablespoons (30ml) wine vinegar
2 tablespoons (30ml) lemon juice
2 tablespoons (30ml) olive oil
1 teaspoon red food colour
6 chicken breasts on bone
SERVES 6

Mix the ingredients together for marinade. Remove the chicken skin. Score flesh and cover with the marinade (taking care to avoid splashing anyone). Marinade for eight hours or overnight. Cook in oven Gas Mark 6, 400F, 200C, or better still, barbecue for approximately 20 minutes until the outside of the chicken is lightly crisp. Serve with green salad and finger bowls.

TURKEY CINZANO

4 thick turkey escalopes or breast fillets
Salt and pepper
Garlic powder
1 oz (25g) butter or margarine
15 oz (425g) tin of tomatoes
1 tablespoon (15ml) tomato puree
4 fl oz (100ml) Cinzano
2 teaspoons lemon juice
2 bay leaves
Parsley and lemon slices, to garnish.
SERVES 4

Sprinkle the turkey with salt and pepper and garlic powder. Melt the butter in a pan and fry turkey until brown. Transfer to a shallow casserole. Liquidise or puree the tomatoes and add to the residue in the pan. Add tomato puree, cook until reduced by half and thickened. Add the Cinzano and lemon juice to the pan, bring to the boil, add salt, pepper and garlic powder to taste, then pour over the turkey. Add bay leaves and cover casserole with a lid. Cook for 45-50 minutes at Gas Mark 4, 350F, 180C.

CHICKEN PIE

Oil for frying
1 onion
4 oz (100g) mushrooms
3-4 chicken pieces
Flour for coating
3/4 pint (450ml) milk
Salt and pepper
Bay leaf
Topping
2 lb (1 kilo) potatoes
White sauce
Butter or margarine
Salt and pepper
Parsley for decoration
SERVES 4

Heat oil and gently soften onion. Fry mushrooms. Place these in a casserole dish. Coat chicken pieces in flour and lightly brown on both sides. Cut into chunks and place in dish on top of onions and mushrooms. Pour on 1/4 pint of the milk, add salt and pepper and bay leaf. Cook in moderate oven (Gas Mark 4-5, 350F, 180C) for 30-45 minutes (until tender). Meanwhile boil and mash potatoes. Make the rest of the milk into a white sauce. Take chicken from oven, drain the juice into the white sauce. Arrange chicken and mushrooms and onions in base of serving dish. Add white sauce and top with potatoes. Dot with margarine. Return to oven and brown. Garnish with parsley if liked.

CHICKEN MYERS

4-6 chicken breasts, skinned and boned
8 oz (225g) broccoli
10 1/2 fl oz (298g) condensed cream of chicken soup
4 tablespoons (60ml) real mayonnaise
6 tablespoons (90ml) whipping cream
1/2 level teaspoon (2.5 ml) curry powder
2 oz (50g) Cheddar cheese grated
SERVES 4-6

Cook broccoli for 4-5 minutes, if using frozen thaw first do not cook. Arrange chicken and broccoli in a shallow baking dish. Combine the undiluted chicken soup with the mayonnaise, cream and curry powder. Spoon mixture over chicken and broccoli, then sprinkle with the grated cheese. Bake about 40-45 minutes (Gas Mark 5, 375F, 190C) until chicken is cooked and the cheese is golden brown. Don't overcook or sauce may separate. Halved tomatoes enhance appearance placed down centre of dish before cooking. This is a very quick and easy dish and no one would guess the contents of the sauce.

CHICKEN IN LEMON SAUCE

4 chicken joints, skinned
1 lemon, grated rind and
juice
1 small onion, chopped
1 stick of celery
Thyme, a few sprigs
Salt and pepper
½ pint (300ml) chicken
stock
1 oz (25g) margarine
1 oz (25g) plain flour
Garnish
Watercress
Lemon Twists
SERVES 4

Place the chicken joints in a 3 pint (1.75 litre) casserole. Add the lemon rind, juice, onion, celery, thyme, salt and pepper to taste, to the stock. Pour over the chicken joints. Cover the casserole and cook in a pre-heated, moderately hot oven, Gas Mark 5, 375F, 190C. for an hour until the chicken is tender. Transfer the chicken to a serving dish and keep hot. Strain the stock. Melt the margarine in a small pan and stir in the flour. Cook for 1 minute, remove from the heat and gradually blend in the stock from the chicken. Return to the heat and cook, stirring continuously until thickened. Check the seasoning. Pour over the chicken joints and garnish.

CHICKEN AND LEEK CASSEROLE

Fat for frying or oil
1 small chicken, cut into
joints
4 potatoes, peeled and sliced
2 tablespoons flour
Salt and pepper
Pinch of mixed herbs
3 leeks, sliced
4 tomatoes, peeled and
sliced
2 oz (50g) split peas
(soaked overnight)
½ packet minestrone soup
1½ pints (900ml) water
SERVES 4

Heat fat or oil and fry chicken joints until brown. Put potatoes in ovenproof dish, sprinkle with flour, salt, pepper and herbs. Place chicken joints on top, add remainder of vegetables, mix soup with water and pour over chicken, cover casserole and cook Gas Mark 4, 350F, 180C for 1½-2 hours.

ANNIVERSARY CHICKEN

1 small onion, chopped
A little butter
½ clove of garlic crushed
(optional)
1 tablespoon (15ml)
tomato puree
½ level tablespoon (8ml)
curry powder
2 tablespoons (30ml)
lemon juice
2 tablespoons (30ml)
apricot jam
1 chicken stock cube
¼-½ pint (150-300ml)
good mayonnaise
½-1 lb (225-450g)
chicken or turkey, cooked
8 oz (225g) green or black
grapes seeded and skinned
1½ oz (38g) flaked
almonds
Parsley to garnish
SERVES 6

Prepare the day before needed. Gently fry onion with garlic in the butter until soft, add tomato puree, curry powder and 1 tablespoon (15ml) lemon juice, jam and crumbled cube. Heat gently until jam is melted, then put in blender. Allow to cool and stir in mayonnaise. Fold in chicken, cover and chill overnight. The following day toss in the grapes and the remainder of the lemon juice and the almonds. Serves 6 but more if mixed with pasta (cooked bows look nice).

CHICKEN WITH LYMESWOLD

2 chicken breasts skinned
1 oz (25g) ham chopped
1 oz (25g) Lymeswold or
soft blue cheese
Brown breadcrumbs
Flour
1 egg to coat
2 oz (50g) butter
SERVES 2

Place butter in ovenproof dish, place in oven to melt. Chop ham and cheese together, slit breasts lengthways and fill with ham and cheese. Dust breasts in flour before coating first in egg (beaten) then into breadcrumbs. Place breasts into dish with melted butter and return to heated oven for 25 minutes at Gas Mark 5, 370F, 190C.

CHICKEN WITH APRICOTS AND BRANDY

4 oz (125g) dried apricots
4 to 6 chicken breasts boned
3 level tablespoons (45g)
plain flour
4 oz (125g) English butter
4 tablespoons (60ml) dry
white wine or cider
1-2 tablespoons (15-
30ml) brandy (optional)
4 oz (125g) streaky bacon
chopped
4 oz (125g) mushrooms
wiped and sliced
4 oz (125g) onion skinned
and chopped
½ pint (300ml) chicken
stock
1 bay leaf
Salt and freshly ground
black pepper
3 juniper berries
5 fl oz (150ml) fresh
single cream
4-6 thick round slices of
bread
Fresh parsley or watercress
to garnish
SERVES 4-6

Soak apricots overnight in cold water. Dust the chicken with a little flour. Melt 1½ oz (38g) butter in a heavy frying pan, gently brown chicken on all sides, then remove to a large casserole. Add wine, brandy to the pan, bring to the boil and pour over the chicken. Melt 1½ oz (38g) butter and fry bacon, mushrooms and onions slowly, until soft and onion is going brown. Blend in 3 tablespoons (45g) flour and gradually stir in stock, season well, add juniper berries, apricots and bay leaf. Pour the sauce over the chicken, cover and cook in oven at Gas Mark 3, 325F, 160C, for 1½ hours. Meanwhile, fry the bread in remaining butter until crisp and golden, drain and keep hot. When the chicken is cooked, remove from casserole and keep hot, remove bay leaf, then put sauce into blender and puree it. Add fresh cream, adjust seasoning, reheat without boiling. On a serving dish arrange a chicken breast on each bread crouton and spoon some sauce over each piece. Garnish with parsley or watercress. Serve remaining sauce separately.

CHICKEN AU GRATIN

6 oz (150g) left-over
cooked chicken, roughly
chopped
2 hard boiled eggs, sliced
2 medium tomatoes,
skinned and sliced
½ pint (300ml) cheese
sauce, using 2 oz (50g)
cheese
Breadcrumbs for topping
SERVES 2-3

Place in Pyrex dish layers of chicken, eggs and tomatoes. Pour over cheese sauce. Top with crumbs. Place under hot grill to warm through until browned (about 20 minutes). Serve with rice or salad.

CHICKEN PILAF

6 oz (150g) brown rice,
washed
½ a cooked chicken,
(de-boned and shredded)
8 button mushrooms, whole
or quartered
1 chopped onion
¾ pint (450ml) chicken
stock
Polyunsaturated margarine
or oil for frying
1 large tomato, skinned
and chopped
Black pepper
½ teaspoon turmeric
Sliced tomato and
cucumber, to garnish
SERVES 3

Fry onion in a little oil or margarine until soft. Add rice and mushrooms and stir fry for 2-3 minutes. Pour in stock, bring to the boil and stir in turmeric and seasoning. Simmer for 20 minutes. Stir in chicken and tomato 5 minutes before serving, garnished.

CHINESE CHICKEN STIR FRY

8 oz (200g) chicken breast
8 oz (200g) bean sprouts
2 sticks celery
2 oz (50g) button mushrooms
2 oz (50g) pineapple
chunks and their juice ¼
pint (150ml)
½ small tin of kidney beans
1 tablespoon cornflour
Soy sauce
¼ pint (150ml) chicken stock
1 tablespoon
polyunsaturated oil
Seasoning
SERVES 2

Heat the oil in a sauté pan or frying pan and fry chicken (cut into strips), stirring all the while. Add soy sauce to taste. Add bean sprouts and vegetables (finely chopped) with stock and simmer for 15 minutes. Blend cornflour with juice from pineapple chunks. Stir into the mixture. Serve immediately with boiled rice.

CHICKEN, ORANGE AND HONEY

4 lb (2kg) chicken
3 oranges
2 tablespoons clear honey
¼ pint (150ml) dry white
wine
2 teaspoons paprika
Salt and black pepper
3 tablespoons oil
SERVES 8

Wash and clean the chicken, cut into eight joints. Combine the oil and honey and spread over the outside of the chicken pieces. Sprinkle with paprika, salt and black pepper. Remove the trivet from the grill pan. Place the chicken pieces in the pan. Grate the rind of two oranges and sprinkle over the chicken. Cut the flesh from the oranges and reserve for garnish. Squeeze the juice from the third orange and add to the grill pan with the white wine — but do NOT pour over the chicken. Grill the chicken under a gentle heat for about 30 minutes, turning the pieces every 5 minutes and basting with the juices from the pan. When the chicken is cooked and a glossy golden brown, place in a serving dish and garnish with the orange segments. Serve the sauce remaining in a separate sauce boat. Accompany with boiled rice and a green salad.

Chapter Six

Meat

MATCHSTICK BEEF IN RED WINE

4 oz (125g) mushrooms
1 tablespoon (15ml)
vegetable oil
1½ oz (42g) butter
1 medium onion
1¾ lb (794g) topside beef
cut into match stick strips
2 tablespoons (30ml) plain
flour
Salt, freshly ground black
pepper
½ teaspoon (2.5ml) mixed
dried herbs
1 garlic clove
1 tablespoon (15ml) port
½ pint (284ml) beef stock
¼ pint (142ml) red wine
SERVES 6

Slice the mushrooms and heat in the oil and butter for 2 minutes over moderate heat, then remove from pan. Fry the chopped onions for 3-4 minutes stirring once or twice. Toss the beef in the flour mixed with the salt, pepper and dried herbs. Shake off excess flour from the beef and add the meat to the pan. Fry for 5 minutes, stirring frequently. Stir in the garlic (peeled and chopped), mushrooms, port, stock and wine and bring to the boil. Reduce the heat to low, cover the pan and simmer for 25 minutes. Taste the sauce and adjust the seasoning. Serve with jacket potatoes or new potatoes boiled in their skins and a dish of mixed vegetables. Garnish with fresh herbs such as parsley.

DEVILISH BEEF

3-4 teaspoons (15-20ml)
mustard
2 tablespoons (30ml)
tomato puree
2 tablespoons (30ml)
sunflower oil
2½-3 lb (1125g-1350g)
boned and rolled rib of beef
1 tablespoon (15ml) red
wine vinegar
¼-½ teaspoon (1-2.5ml)
cayenne pepper

Mix the mustard, tomato puree and oil together thoroughly in a bowl. Smear the mixture all over the beef. Put the beef on a plate or dish. Cover loosely with foil or cling film and leave in the refrigerator for at least 8 hours — overnight if possible. Heat the oven to Gas Mark 3, 325F, 160C. Put the beef in a roasting tin and cook in the centre of a moderate oven for 1½-1¾ hours. Cool and then chill for a short while in the refrigerator. Carve into thin slices and arrange on a serving dish. May be served with salad in Winter or Summer. Also useful for picnics.

PAM'S CHOW MEIN

2 oz (50g) butter or fat
for frying
1 medium onion
1 lb (450g) minced beef
1 teaspoon curry powder,
heaped
1 teaspoon turmeric, heaped
(optional)
1 teaspoon sugar
½ teaspoon salt
1 oz (25g) sultanas
¼ lb (100g) green beans,
sliced (fresh or frozen)
1 packet chicken noodle
soup mix
15 fl oz boiling water
1 small hard white cabbage
SERVES 4

Melt fat in large frying pan. Chop onion and fry gently for 3 minutes. Add mince to pan and break it down with a fork to remove lumps. When mince is lightly browned add spices and mix in thoroughly. Fry for 1 minute. Add sugar, seasoning, sultanas and beans. Stir well. Add chicken noodle soup mix and pour on the water. Stir again and cover with a lid. Allow to simmer gently while you shred the cabbage very finely to resemble flat noodles. Cover the mince mixture with the shredded cabbage and replace lid. Simmer until the cabbage is just tender (about 30 minutes). Serve with rice or chips or jacket potatoes. This dish can be extended to serve 6 by adding a second packet of chicken noodle soup with an extra cup of water and more cabbage topping. It will not spoil if left cooking for longer than 30 minutes, but should be stirred underneath and water added if the meat starts to stick to the pan. As a "One-Pan-Top-of-Stove" meal it is economical and tasty.

CORNISH PASTIES

½ lb (225g) potatoes
(raw) finely diced
¾ lb (350g) minced steak
or diced skirt
1 medium onion finely
chopped
3 tablespoons water
Salt and pepper
1 lb (450g) shortcrust
pastry
SERVES 4-6

Mix potatoes, meat, onion, water and seasoning. Roll out pastry and cut rounds with a saucer. Wet the edges of the pastry and put about 1 tablespoon of mixture on each round. Fold over and press edges of the pastry together and flute with fingers. Brush with beaten egg or milk. Bake at Gas Mark 8, 450F, 230C for about 15 minutes reducing to Gas Mark 4, 350F, 180C for about one hour altogether.

SWEET AND SOUR BEEF CASSEROLE

1-1½ lb (675g) stewing beef
1 oz (25g) cornflour
Salt and pepper
2 tablespoons (30ml) corn oil
3 fl oz (85ml) cider vinegar
½ green pepper, sliced
1 medium carrot, diced
1 courgette, sliced
½ pint (284ml) water (approx.)
3 oz (75g) brown sugar
1 small tin pineapple pieces with juice
1 small tin bean sprouts, drained
2 teaspoons Worcester sauce
2 teaspoons Soy sauce
SERVES 4-6

Cut meat into strips and coat in cornflour seasoned with salt and pepper. Heat oil and brown meat. Add all the other ingredients and bring to the boil, stirring. Cover and cook at Gas Mark 3, 325F, 160C, for 1½-2 hours until meat is tender. Serve with boiled rice and crispy rolls.

BEEF CURRY

1 oz (25g) dripping
1 lb (450g) beef steak
1 oz (25g) flour
1 level teaspoon salt
1 medium onion, sliced
1 apple, chopped
1 tomato
½ pint (300ml) beef stock or water
Juice of half a lemon
1 level tablespoon curry powder
1 tablespoon sultanas
SERVES 4

Cut the meat into cubes and coat in seasoned flour. Fry in the dripping with the apple, onion and tomato. Add the curry powder and remaining flour and mix well then stir in the stock. Simmer about 2 hours, add sultanas and lemon juice. Serve with boiled rice.

BEEF AND BEAN HOT POT

1 tin butter beans, drained
12 oz (330g) trimmed
and diced stewing steak
½ oz (12g)
polyunsaturated margarine
or 1 tablespoon oil
1 oz (25g) wholemeal
flour
1 lb (1 kilo) potatoes,
peeled and sliced
3 medium carrots, chopped
1 large onion, chopped
½ pint (200ml) beef stock
1 teaspoon Worcester sauce
1 bay leaf
Seasoning to taste
SERVES 4

Season the flour and use to coat the meat. Melt margarine or heat oil in pan and seal meat, stirring well. Add carrots, onion, beef stock and bring to boil stirring continuously. Add the sauce, butter beans and bay leaf. Transfer ingredients to ovenproof dish. Cover and bake for an hour and a half at Gas Mark 5, 375F, 190C. Remove bay leaf. Arrange sliced potatoes over casserole and bake for a further 30 minutes at Gas Mark 6, 400F, 200C or until potatoes are cooked. Any beans can be used in this recipe for variety, e.g. kidney beans, haricot beans etc.

BEEF STROGANOFF

1 oz (25g) margarine or oil
1 onion, chopped
1 lb (500g) rump steak,
surplus fat removed, cut
into inch strips
1 tablespoon flour and
seasoning (salt, pepper,
nutmeg)
4 oz (100g) sliced
mushrooms
½ pint (300ml) beef stock
3 teaspoons tomato puree
2 tablespoons low fat
natural yoghurt
SERVES 4

Sauté onions in oil or margarine until tender. Coat meat in seasoned flour and cook in oil for 8-10 minutes until browned. Add remaining ingredients, except yoghurt, and bring to the boil, stirring well. Just before serving, stir in yoghurt.

CHINESE STEAK

1 lb (450g) frying steak
cut into 1 inch cubes
Butter or margarine for
frying
Pepper and salt
3 oz (75g) chopped
pineapple
3 oz (75g) piccalilli
1 teaspoon soy sauce
½ pint (300ml) water
2 teaspoons oil
2 tablespoons vinegar
1 ½ tablespoons tomato
puree
1 dessertspoon cornflour
2 oz (50g) finely chopped
onion
SERVES 4

Heat fat in frying pan and fry steak on all sides. Heat oil in a small pan and add the onion and fry lightly. Add the water, pineapple, piccalilli, sugar and tomato puree. Blend the cornflour with the vinegar and soy sauce. Add to the pan and stir well. Leave to simmer for 15 minutes. Add steak cubes and heat for a few minutes. Serve immediately with plain boiled rice.

CORNED BEEF HASH

1 lb (500g) potatoes
2 large onions
1 tablespoon oil
1 oz (25g) butter
Salt and pepper
½ teaspoon dried herbs
8 oz (200g) tin tomatoes
7 oz (200g) tin corned
beef
6 oz (150g) mature
Cheddar cheese, grated
4 oz (100g) crushed corn
flakes
SERVES 3-4

Cut potatoes into half inch cubes. Chop onions. Heat oil and butter in a large frying pan, add potatoes and onion. Fry gently for 5 minutes. Season, add herbs and tomatoes. Cover and cook for 10 minutes until potatoes are tender. Add cubed corned beef. Cover and cook for 5 minutes. Mix cheese and cornflakes, sprinkle over top and brown under hot grill.

LASAGNE

Sauce
4 oz (125g) margarine
4 oz (125g) flour
1 level teaspoon dried mustard
Salt and pepper
2 pints (1130ml) milk
4 oz (125g) grated cheese
Filling
1 lb (450g) cooked mince
9 sheets/6 oz (175g) lasagne, uncooked
Topping
4 oz (125g) grated cheese
SERVES 8

First prepare the sauce (see sauces section). Make 3 layers each of cooked mince and uncooked lasagne, cheese sauce. Start with mince and end with sauce. Sprinkle remaining cheese on top. Bake at Gas Mark 5, 375F, 190C. for 45-50 minutes. This is better assembled and baked shortly before use. But sauce, mince etc. can be put ready sooner.

SAVOURY MEAT PIE

8 oz (225g) shortcrust pastry
1 sliced onion
2 tablespoons butter
1 tablespoon curry powder
1 teaspoon sugar
1 teaspoon salt
1 tablespoon vinegar
1 tablespoon chutney
3/4 lb (350g) raw mincemeat
1 sliced bread soaked in 3/4 cup milk.
SERVES 5

Fry onion in butter, add curry powder, sugar, salt, vinegar, chutney and meat. Draw milk from bread (save milk) mash with fork and add to mixture. Add one beaten egg, mix well and set aside. Roll out pastry and put in a 9 inch flan tin. Turn filling into pastry case. Beat second egg with saved milk (approx. half a cup), season and pour gently over mixture. Dot with butter. Bake at Gas Mark 6, 400F, 200C for 10 minutes, reduce to Gas Mark 4, 350F, 180C and bake for another 20-25 minutes.

SAUSAGE AND MINCE PLAIT

*Large packet of frozen puff
pastry*
Filling
8 oz (200g) sausagemeat
8 oz (200g) mince
Onion
*2 tablespoons (30ml)
tomato puree*
Mushroom (optional)
Salt and pepper
*Pinch curry powder
(optional)*
SERVES 8

Mix all above and pre-cook in frying pan for 10 minutes. Leave to cool after mixing well. Roll out pastry as big as you can make it. Straighten edges. Lay meat mixture down centre leaving top and bottom clear. Cut sides and plait as usual. Brush with egg and cook (Gas Mark 7, 425F, 220C) for 45 minutes until browned.

SHEPHERD'S PIE

*1 lb-1 ½ lb (450g-675g)
potatoes*
*1 lb (450g) minced lamb
or beef*
1 ½ oz (38g) fat
1 onion, finely chopped
*½ pint (300ml) stock or
water*
1 oz (25g) flour
Salt and pepper
1 oz (25g) butter
2 tablespoons milk
SERVES 4-6

Peel and boil potatoes, heat the fat and fry the onions lightly. Add the minced meat, if raw brown lightly, cover with stock, simmer for 30 minutes and thicken with flour, mixed to a paste with a little water, and boil again for 3 minutes. If meat is already cooked, omit simmering for 30 minutes. Season to taste, drain potatoes and mash with milk and butter, season to taste. When the mince has cooled place in an ovenproof dish, cover with potatoes and place in oven for around 30 minutes at Gas Mark 5, 375F, 190C.

STEAK AND KIDNEY PIE

1 lb (450g) stewing beef
¼ lb (125g) kidney
Flour, salt and pepper
1 oz (25g) dripping or oil
1 small onion (optional),
chopped
½ pint (300ml) stock or
water
Shortcrust or flaky pastry
SERVES 4-6

Melt dripping in heavy saucepan, brown the cubed beef and kidney after rolling in the seasoned flour. Add the onion and then the stock and simmer until tender, 1½-2 hours. Cool, put into pie dish with funnel in the middle if large, wet the edges of the dish and line with pastry strips. Cover with crust and flake the edges. Make a hole in the middle and brush with egg or milk. Bake at Gas Mark 7, 425F, 210C for 30-35 minutes.

STEAK AND MUSHROOM PIE

As steak and kidney, replacing the kidney with 2 oz (50g) of sliced mushrooms.

STEAK AND KIDNEY PUDDING

1 lb (450g) stewing steak
¼ lb (125g) kidney
Small onion, finely chopped
Flour, salt and pepper
½ lb (225g) suet crust
pastry
SERVES 4-6

Cut steak into thin strips and roll in seasoned flour and cut kidney into small pieces. Make suet crust pastry with 8 oz (225g) self raising flour, 3 oz (75g) shredded suet, salt and water to mix. Roll out two thirds of the mixture and line a well greased basin. Put the meat in and half fill the basin with stock or water. Cover with the remaining one third suet crust and cover with grease proof paper. Steam for 3 hours.

LAMB KEBABS WITH TOMATO SAUCE

12 oz (300g) leg of lamb, remove fat and cut into 1½ inch (4cm) cubes
4 small tomatoes, halved
4 oz (200g) button mushrooms
1 green pepper, deseeded and cut into 1 inch squares
Sauce
1 oz (25g) polyunsaturated margarine
1 onion, finely chopped
14 oz (400g) tin tomatoes, chopped
1 oz (25g) flour, blended with juice from tomatoes
¼ pint (150ml) cider
½ pint (300ml) water
1 beef stock cube
2 teaspoons sugar
4 teaspoons vinegar
½ teaspoon Worcestershire sauce
Seasoning
SERVES 4

Arrange lamb, tomatoes, mushrooms and pepper on four long or eight short skewers. Brush with polyunsaturated oil. Season and place under grill for 10-12 minutes, turning regularly. For the sauce melt the margarine and slowly sauté onion for 10 minutes. Remove from heat, add all remaining ingredients and bring to the boil. Simmer for 20 minutes, stir occasionally and serve with kebabs. Kebabs are normally served on a bed of hot rice.

CREAMY PORK TILBERTHWAITE

1 tablespoon (15ml)
cooking oil
1 lb (400g) lean pork
(steak or fillet)
4 oz (100g) cooking apple
finely sliced
4 oz (100g) onion finely
sliced
10.4 oz (295g) tin
concentrated mushroom
soup
Ground black or white
peppercorns
Minimal salt (as the soup
is well salted)
Worcestershire sauce
SERVES 3-4

Preheat oven and heat oil in a deep saucepan. Cut pork into half-inch thick chunks, removing any surplus fat. Seal in the hot oil on all sides. Spread a third of the soup on the base of an ovenproof dish; add half the sliced apple and onion, season and dot with Worcestershire sauce. Arrange the pork pieces on top and cover with the remaining apple and onion. Cover with the rest of the soup, season with salt and pepper and "dot" with Worcestershire sauce. Cover tightly with a lid or aluminium foil and cook at Gas Mark 4, 350F, 180C for 1 hour 15-30 minutes. After cooking, sprinkle with chopped parsley or browned breadcrumbs, and serve with a green vegetable and rice, or jacket or roast potatoes. Extra refinement if time permits; keeping the pork hot, liquidise the sauce until smooth, reheat and add a dollop of cream, before pouring over the pork.

SWEET AND SOUR PORK CHOPS

8 oz (200g) brown rice
4 lean pork chops
8 oz (200g) tin pineapple
pieces, in own juice
1 chopped green pepper
1 onion, chopped
2 inch (5cm) pieces of
peeled and diced cucumber
1 medium carrot, grated
1 teaspoon sugar
2 tablespoons soy sauce
1½ tablespoons wine vinegar
2 tablespoons tomato puree
2 teaspoons cornflour
Polyunsaturated oil
SERVES 4

Put the pork chops to grill. Cook the rice in boiling salted water. Drain, refresh and keep hot. Drain off pineapple juice and make up to a quarter of a pint with water. Heat 2 tablespoons oil in frying pan. Cook onion, pepper, cucumber and carrot for 2-3 minutes, stirring well. Stir in soy sauce, sugar, wine vinegar, tomato puree and pineapple/water liquid. Stirring continuously, bring to the boil. Blend the cornflour with a little water and add to the pan. Cook until thickened. Arrange the rice on a serving dish, with chops around. Pour the sauce over and serve at once.

PORK FILLET IN PUFF PASTRY

12 oz (340g) bought or
home-made puff pastry
3 medium fillets of pork or
2 large fillets
4 oz (125g) mushrooms
3 fl oz (100ml) dry white
wine
Salt and pepper to season
1 sprig of rosemary
1 small egg
SERVES 6

Roll out the puff pastry very thinly into a long panel. Cut rectangles to enclose the chosen fillets of pork, being sure that each is large enough to envelope the fillet loosely and with a ¾ inch overlap at the centre top. Lay one fillet centrally on each rectangle. Season lightly with salt and pepper. Strew thinly sliced, unpeeled mushrooms equally over the fillets. Strip the sprig of rosemary of its spiked leaves, pound resolutely until reduced to a complete pulp and then mix with wine. Drip mixture equally over the fillets. Beat and strain the egg and brush over all pastry edges. Overlap the ends and pinch together firmly. If desired, refrigerate overnight. Immediately before baking brush all upper pastry surfaces with strained beaten egg. Bake one shelf above the centre of the oven at Gas Mark 6, 400F, 200C, until the pastry is a rich, golden brown (35 to 40 minutes).

MEDALLIONS OF PORK

1½ lb (675g) pork fillet
1 oz (25g) butter
1 tablespoon (15ml) oil
2 small onions, sliced
1 tablespoon (15ml) paprika
2 tablespoons (2x15ml)
plain flour
4 tablespoons (4x15ml)
amontillado sherry
½ pint (300ml) stock
4 oz (100g) button
mushrooms, halved
6 tablespoons (6x15ml)
single cream
Salt and pepper
SERVES 6

Cut pork into half-inch thick slices and fry both sides briskly in the butter and oil. Take out the pork, stir in onions and paprika, cook for a few seconds then stir in the flour. Add the sherry and stock. Put the pork back into the pan, bring to the boil and simmer very gently for 30-40 minutes. Add the mushrooms for the last 10 minutes. Stir in the cream and season with salt and pepper if necessary.

SWEET AND SOUR PORK

1½ lb (675g) shoulder pork
1 oz (25g) butter or
margarine
1 small onion, peeled and
chopped
1 tablespoon (rounded)
plain flour
8 oz (225g) tin pineapple,
slices
1 small green pepper,
deseeded and sliced
2 tablespoons (level) brown
sugar
2 teaspoons tomato sauce
2 teaspoons Worcester sauce
2 tablespoons vinegar
1 tablespoon (level) mango
chutney or sweet pickle
8 oz (225g) long grain
rice
SERVES 4

Cut meat into 1 inch cubes. Melt fat in a saucepan. Add onion and meat and fry for 5 minutes. Stir in flour. Strain pineapple syrup into a measuring jug. Make up to half a pint with water. Stir pineapple syrup, sliced pepper, brown sugar, tomato sauce, Worcester sauce, vinegar, chutney and half a level teaspoon of salt into the saucepan. Bring to the boil, cover and simmer for 40-50 minutes until the meat is tender. Cut 2 slices of pineapple into small pieces and add to the pork mixture. Cook rice in boiling salted water 10-12 minutes until tender. Drain and rinse under hot water. Serve rice and pork mixture on a warmed dish. Garnish with reserved pineapple slices.

PORK CHOPS IN CIDER

4 pork chops
1 lemon
2 oz (50g) sultanas
1 large apple
2 oz (50g) butter
1 dessertspoon flour
¼ pint (150ml) cider
SERVES 4

Melt the butter and brown the chops on both sides, then place in an ovenproof dish. Add the flour to the fat in the pan and brown gently, stirring all the time. Add the cider, lemon juice and grated rind, sultanas and diced apple. Season well and pour over chops. Cook at Gas Mark 4, 350F, 180C for 45 minutes to 1 hour.

SPICY SAUSAGE PIE

½ lb (225g) pastry, ideally
wholewheat
(Ordinary shortcrust can
be used)
8 oz (225g) sausage meat
1 finely chopped onion
1 teaspoon (5ml) oregano
2 tablespoons (30ml)
tomato ketchup
Salt and pepper to taste
3 hard boiled eggs
SERVES 4-6

Slice the eggs thinly. Mix together onion, oregano, ketchup, seasoning and sausagemeat. Roll out half the pastry and line base of shallow, ovenproof plate, trim edges and brush with egg and milk. Put on half sausagemeat mixture and place eggs over. Cover eggs carefully with rest of sausagemeat mixture. Roll out rest of pastry to cover. Trim and cook for 40-45 minutes. at Gas Mark 6, 400F, 200C.

SAUSAGE AND EGG PIE

6 oz (175g) shortcrust
pastry
½ oz (13g) butter
3 oz (75g) bacon, derinded
and chopped
4 oz (125g) mushrooms,
chopped
1 lb (450g) sausagemeat
½ small onion, finely
chopped
2 teaspoons chopped parsley
4 eggs
SERVES 4-6

Roll out pastry and line 8 inch pie plate. Fry the bacon, onions and mushrooms in the butter until starting to brown. Add the sausagemeat and fry for 10 minutes stirring frequently, then add the parsley. Spread in the pastry case. Beat the eggs and season then pour over the sausage mixture. Bake at Gas Mark 7, 425F, 210C for 40-50 minutes. Serve hot or cold.

GLAZED HAM

Middle or corner gammon
(approx. 4 lb (2 kg))
2 pints (1 litre) water
1 large onion
1 bay leaf
6 peppercorns
3 oz (75g) soft brown
sugar
2 teaspoons dry mustard
Cloves

Soak gammon overnight in cold water. Put into saucepan with 2 pints of fresh cold water with quartered onion, bay leaf and peppercorns and cover. Bring to the boil and simmer for 1½ to 2 hours. Peel off the skin and mark fat in diamond pattern with a sharp knife. Place in roasting tin and press the mixed sugar and mustard on to the fat, then put a clove in the diamonds. Bake at Gas Mark 7, 425F, 210C, until fat is crisp, about 15-20 minutes.

SAVOURY LOAF

1 egg
6 oz (175g) lentils
½ lb (225g) streaky bacon
or bits
1½ lb (675g) sausagemeat
1 medium onion
Salt and pepper
3 hard boiled eggs
SERVES 6

Rinse lentils, put in pan of cold water and bring to the boil. Boil for 15 minutes, drain well. Peel and grate onion in bowl, cut up bacon and add also sausagemeat and one egg. Beat well, beat in lentils. Line 2 lb loaf tin with greaseproof paper. Put in half mixture, put hard boiled eggs down centre. Cover with remaining mixture. Cover with greased paper, bake for 1½ to 2 hours at Gas Mark 2, 300F, 150C. Stand tin in water, leave in tin till cold, then turn out.

CELERY AND HAM GRATIN

6 canned celery hearts
6 slices ham
French mustard
½ pint (300ml) white sauce
¼ pint (150ml) double cream
1 egg yolk
Seasoning
4 oz (100g) grated cheese
6 whole tomatoes, sliced
SERVES 6

Roll each heart of celery in a slice of ham, spread with mustard. Place in a shallow ovenproof buttered dish. Heat sauce, stir in cream, egg yolk, seasoning and three quarters of the cheese. Spoon over the celery and ham. Arrange the tomatoes on top and sprinkle with remaining cheese. Place under a moderate grill until heated through and top is golden.

MACARONI SNACK

4 oz (100g) macaroni
2 oz (50g) smoked bacon
1 medium sized onion
3 oz (75g) Cheddar cheese
1 oz (25g) cornflour
1 oz (25g) butter
¼ pint (150ml) milk
1 tablespoon white
breadcrumbs
SERVES 2

Cook macaroni in salted boiling water for about 15 minutes. Drain. Fry chopped bacon. Sweat sliced onion in butter until soft. Add bacon and cornflour. Mix well, then gradually add milk until thickened, then stir in cheese reserving a little to add to breadcrumbs for topping. Mix in the cooked macaroni and turn into an ovenproof dish. Add the topping of cheese and breadcrumbs and brown under the grill.

TAGLIATELLE WITH HAM AND CREAM SAUCE

1 lb (450g) dried, green
tagliatelle (tagliatelle
verdi)
1 tablespoon (15ml) oil
1 onion, finely chopped
4 oz (100g) mushrooms,
sliced
Salt and ground black
pepper
4 oz (100g) cooked ham,
cut in strips
½ pint (300ml) single
cream
6 rashers of streaky bacon,
grilled and chopped
SERVES 6

Cook the tagliatelle in a large pan of boiling, salted water for 10 minutes. Drain and put the tagliatelle on a hot serving dish, and keep warm. Heat the oil in frying pan, fry the onion until soft, about 5 minutes. Add mushrooms and a little black pepper and fry for a further 3 minutes. Add ham and heat gently. Gradually stir in the cream maintaining the gentle heat. Pour the sauce over the tagliatelle. Garnish with the chopped crisp bacon and serve immediately with a green salad.

STIR FRIED LIVER

2 tablespoons (30ml)
cornflour
2 tablespoons (30ml) soy
sauce
1 lb (450g) lamb's liver
3 tablespoons (45g)
vegetable oil
1 bunch spring onions
1 green pepper
Salt and pepper
2 tablespoons (30ml)
sherry
2 teaspoons (10ml) caster
sugar
5 tablespoons (75ml)
chicken stock
SERVES 4

Mix cornflour and soy sauce together. Cut liver
into strips and coat with cornflour mix. Heat
oil and add liver and fry 30 seconds turning.
Add chopped onions and sliced pepper and cook
for a further 4-5 minutes over a high heat. Add
seasoning, sherry, sugar and stock. Cook for a
further minute. Throughout use high heat and
stir frequently. Serve with Chinese noodles or
rice.

SPRING LAMB CASSEROLE

4 lamb cutlets
1 ½ tablespoons oil
1 small onion, sliced
1 small stick celery, sliced
3 carrots, sliced
8 small button onions
½ oz (15g) plain flour
½ pint (250ml) chicken
stock
Browning to colour
Bouquet garni
Salt and pepper
2 small dessert apples
Chopped parsley
SERVES 4

Sauté the lamb cutlets in the oil until brown.
Remove the cutlets and add all the vegetables.
Cook for 3-4 minutes, add the flour and then
the stock. Bring to the boil stirring well and add
the browning, bouquet garni and seasoning. Put
in casserole, replace the cutlets and cook in
moderate oven for one hour at Gas Mark 3,
325F, 160C. Add the peeled, sliced apples and
cook for a further 10 minutes. Garnish with
chopped parsley. Serve with boiled new potatoes
and spring cabbage.

MINTY LAMB STEW

1½ lb (675g) stewing
lamb, cubed
2 large onions, sliced
2 or 3 large tomatoes,
skinned and chopped
1-2 cloves of garlic chopped
1 large handful of fresh mint
Juice of 1 lemon
¾-1 pint (450-600ml)
good stock
Salt and pepper
SERVES 6

Place all the ingredients into a large casserole. Bring to the boil on the top of the stove, then transfer casserole to the oven and simmer in a low oven for 1½-2 hours until tender. Alternatively cook in a slow cooker for 2 hours until tender. Serve with new potatoes and carrots.

RACK OF LAMB IN PASTRY WITH WALNUTS

Rack of lamb (8 chops)
Salt and black pepper
Butter
1 onion, finely chopped
3 tablespoons (45ml) of
olive oil
8 oz (225g) mushrooms,
finely chopped
2 slices of cooked ham,
finely chopped
4 oz (100g) walnuts,
coarsely chopped
8 oz (225g) puff pastry
1 egg yolk, beaten
SERVES 4

Trim off fat from lamb. Separate meat from bone and chine bone. Season with salt and pepper. Brush with softened butter and roast in moderate oven Gas Mark 5, 375F, 190C for 20 minutes or until the lamb is half cooked, and allow to cool quickly. Sauté onions in 3 tablespoons (45ml) each of butter and olive oil until onion is transparent. Add mushrooms and cook stirring constantly until mixture is dry. Add chopped ham and walnuts. Season to taste and cook for a further minute. Allow to cool. Spread lamb with mixture, brush all over with softened butter. Roll out puff pastry into thin sheet and wrap lamb in it allowing bones to protrude from pastry. Decorate with leaves cut from trimmings, fix on with beaten egg. Brush over pastry with water and cover loosely with foil. Place lamb on baking sheet and bake in hot oven Gas Mark 8, 450F, 230C. Remove foil. Brush pastry now with beaten egg yolk. Continue baking 15 minutes or until cooked and brown.

LAMB COBBLER

1 ½ lb (675g) boneless lean stewing lamb, cubed
Seasoned flour to coat
2 tablespoons (30ml) oil
1 large onion, chopped
2 carrots, diced
1 stalk celery, chopped
¾ pint (450ml) stock
1 tablespoon (15ml) tomato puree
½ teaspoon (2.5ml) finely chopped fresh or dried rosemary
Cobbler
8 oz (225g) self raising flour
Pinch of salt
2 oz (50g) butter or margarine
½ teaspoon (2.5ml) dried or 1 teaspoon finely chopped fresh rosemary
6 tablespoons (90ml) milk to glaze
SERVES 4

Toss the lamb in seasoned flour and set aside. Heat the oil in a frying pan and cook the onion, carrot and celery over a low heat until beginning to soften, about 3-5 minutes. Remove with a slotted spoon and place in a 3 pint casserole. Add the meat to the pan juices and brown on all sides. Transfer to the casserole. Pour the stock into the pan juices and bring to the boil. Pour over the meat and vegetables in the casserole. Stir in the tomato puree and rosemary. Cover and cook in a moderate oven Gas Mark 4, 350F, 180C, for about 1 hour. Meanwhile make the cobbler topping. Sift the flour and salt into a bowl, rub in the butter or margarine, stir in the rosemary and mix to a soft but workable dough with the milk. Roll out the dough on a floured board to about ¾ inch thick. Cut into rounds using a 2 inch plain or fluted cutter. Place on a greased baking tray and glaze with milk. Bake in a hot oven Gas Mark 7, 425F, 220C for 15 minutes until well risen and golden brown. Place on top of the casserole and cook for a further 5 minutes. Serve at once.

IRISH STEW

1 ½ lb (675g) middle neck of mutton
2 lb (900g) potatoes
2 large onions
Salt and pepper
Cold water
SERVES 4

Trim the meat of excess fat and cut into pieces for serving. Peel and chop onions and potatoes and place alternate layers in a pan or ovenproof casserole. Add water to about ½-¾ full. Cover and bring to the boil then simmer until tender, 2 hours. Oven Gas Mark 2, 300F, 150C.

LAMB CHOPS A L'ORANGE

4 chump lamb chops
5 oz (150g) orange
marmalade
½ oz (13g) butter
1 tablespoon dry sherry
1 small clove garlic
(optional)
Salt
SERVES 4

Heat the marmalade, butter, sherry and garlic (skinned and finely chopped) and salt, stirring occasionally until marmalade is melted. Grill the chops at medium heat for 10-15 minutes, brushing them with the marmalade mixture 2-3 times each side. Serve in heated dish with remaining sauce poured over.

BAKED LAMB CHOPS

4 loin chops
1 oz (25g) fat
2 onions
Small tin tomatoes
1 level teaspoon sugar
Salt and pepper
2 oz (50g) grated cheese
2 oz (50g) fresh
breadcrumbs
SERVES 4

Trim excess fat off the chops and remove bone. Peel and slice onions. Brown the chops in the hot fat. Place in a shallow ovenproof dish and put onion on top of each chop. Pour over tomatoes and add seasoning and sugar. Mix cheese and breadcrumbs and sprinkle thickly over the chops. Cover and bake slowly at Gas Mark 3, 325F, 170C for 1½ hours.

ROAST LEG OF LAMB

4 lb (2kg) leg of lamb
3 juniper berries
2 level teaspoon dry
mustard
2 teaspoons water
4 tablespoons Gin
(optional)
6 oz (175g) redcurrant
jelly
2 tablespoons flour
¼ level teaspoon salt
SERVES 6-8

Crush the juniper berries and mustard, water and seasoning and spread over lamb. Roast lamb at Gas Mark 4, 350F, 180C for about 2½ hours until cooked. Put on heated serving dish. Drain excess fat from roasting tin and add half a pint of water and bring to the boil, stirring to gather all sediment and juices. Make up to ¾ pint in saucepan add gin, redcurrant jelly and flour thickening and cook until thickened.

Chapter Seven

Vegetables

RATATOUILLE

2 tablespoons (30ml) oil
1 oz (25g) butter
1 large onion, thinly sliced
1 garlic clove, finely
chopped
8 oz (200g) tomatoes,
skinned and chopped
2 medium green peppers
16 oz (500g) courgettes
2 medium aubergines
1 teaspoon (5ml) salt
Salt and pepper to taste
4 tablespoons (60ml)
chopped parsley

Heat oil and butter in a large saucepan. Add onion and garlic and fry gently until slightly coloured. Add tomatoes and sliced peppers and cover pan. Slice courgettes and thinly slice aubergines and add to pan together with parsley and seasoning. Cover and simmer very gently for approximately 1 hour, or bake in a hot oven for the same time.

SPICY MARROW WITH GINGER

1½-2 lb (675-900g)
medium-sized marrow (or
courgettes may be used)
1 onion, peeled and chopped
2 tablespoons olive oil or
sunflower oil
1-2 teaspoons ground
ginger
2 oz (50g) crystallised or
stem ginger or ginger
conserve
Freshly ground black pepper
Sea salt
Chopped fresh coriander or
parsley
SERVES 4-6

Peel marrow, then cut into even sized pieces about 1 inch long and ¾ inch thick; do not remove seed if tender. Fry onion in oil in medium sized heavy based pan for 5 minutes. Add marrow, ground and chopped ginger or ginger conserve. Cover and cook gently for 15-20 minutes until marrow is nearly tender. Take off the lid and let mixture boil for 5-10 minutes until the liquid has evaporated. Season and sprinkle with chopped coriander or parsley. Cook for 30-35 minutes.

RED HOT CABBAGE

1 small red cabbage
1 ½ oz (40g) butter
1 small onion very finely chopped
1 large cooking apple, peeled, cored and sliced
½ teaspoon salt
Boiling water
2 tablespoons red wine
2 tablespoons brown sugar
SERVES 6-8

Remove coarse outer leaves. Cut the cabbage in half and take out the hard centre stalk. Wash thoroughly, shred finely and place in a large saucepan. Sprinkle a tablespoon of salt over the red cabbage. Cover with boiling water. Leave for a few minutes, then drain off all the water. Melt the butter in a large pan and sauté the chopped onion for about 2-3 minutes. Add the moist cabbage, salt and apples and cook rapidly for about 5 minutes in 1 inch of boiling water. Cover, reduce heat and allow to simmer for 15-20 minutes when most of the water will be absorbed and cabbage tender. Stir in wine and sugar and simmer for a further 8-10 minutes. Serve hot.

GRATIN DAUPHINOIS

1 oz (25g) softened butter
2 lb (900g) potatoes, sliced thinly
1 large onion, finely chopped
½ lb (225g) Gruyere cheese, grated
Salt and pepper
¼ pint (142ml) single cream
Nutmeg
SERVES 4

Brush sides of dish with part of butter. Layer a quarter of the potatoes overlapping and dot with butter. Sprinkle a quarter of onion on top of potatoes then add quarter of cheese and salt and pepper. Pour over a quarter of the cream. Continue in layers finishing with remaining cheese and cream. Cover with lid (or buttered greaseproof paper or foil). Bake in medium oven Gas Mark 5, 375F, 190C, for 1 hour. Brown under preheated hot grill for 5 minutes until bubbling.

BRAISED TURNIPS

1 lb (500g) turnips
2 tablespoons (30ml) oil
¼ pint (150ml) chicken stock
1 tablespoon (15ml) tomato puree
1 tablespoon (15ml) creamed horseradish or horseradish sauce
SERVES 4

Peel turnips and cut into half-inch cubes. Fry briskly in oil until starting to brown. Add chicken stock and bring to the boil. Add tomato puree and horseradish and simmer for 30 minutes. Can be cooked in the microwave in a suitable lidded container for 15 minutes at 50 per cent power (650 watt oven). Particularly delicious with roast beef and ham and bacon dishes.

PARSNIP CHIPS

Cook small pieces of parsnips in salted water for 10-15 minutes. Drain and dry well. Deep fry for 5 minutes. Sprinkle with grated parmesan or cheddar cheese.

DUCHESS VEGETABLES

1 lb (450g) potatoes
8 oz (225g) carrots
Salt and pepper
½ oz (12g) butter
half an egg
SERVES 4-6

Boil vegetables separately until cooked. Drain and mash separately until smooth. Mix vegetables together. Season to taste and add butter and egg mixing well. Using a forcing bag pipe about 12 pyramids onto a greased tray. Bake at Gas Mark 4, 350F, 180C for 30-35 minutes. Will freeze on tray, cook from frozen 40-45 minutes.

TOMATOES AND BASIL WITH CRISP POTATO TOPPING

1 lb (450g) potatoes
½ oz (12g) margarine
2-3 tablespoons (30-45ml) skimmed milk
14 oz (400g) tin of tomatoes, drained
2 teaspoons (10ml) fresh basil
2 oz (50g) Cheddar cheese, grated
SERVES 6

Cream boiled potatoes with the margarine and skimmed milk, seasoned with a little black pepper. Place tomatoes in an ovenproof dish, sprinkle with the basil, then top with the creamed potato and the grated cheese. Bake in a moderate oven for 25 minutes.

CRISPY POTATOES

1 lb (450g) potatoes parboiled
¼ pint (150ml) plain fromage frais
2 tablespoons (30ml) milk
1 egg
Salt and pepper to taste
2 oz (50g) Double Gloucester cheese, grated
SERVES 2

Slice potatoes and arrange in an ovenproof dish. Beat fromage frais with the milk and egg, season, then pour over the potatoes. Sprinkle liberally with grated cheese. Cook for about 30 minutes at Gas Mark 6, 400F, 200C.

BRAISED FENNEL

2 heads fennel
¾ pint (425ml) chicken stock
1 oz (25g) butter
1 level tablespoon plain flour
SERVES 4

Trim fennel and cut lengthways, simmer in stock until just tender. Strain well and keep hot, reserving stock. Blend softened butter and flour into stock and boil, stirring continuously until thickened. Pour over fennel and serve at once.

BROAD BEANS WITH BACON

1 lb (450g) shelled broad beans
1 rasher bacon, diced
1 small onion, chopped finely
1 oz (25g) butter
1/4 pint (150ml) chicken stock
Salt and pepper
SERVES 4-6

Fry bacon and onion in butter without browning, until onion is soft. Add beans and stock, cover and simmer for about 15 minutes until cooked and most of the stock has evaporated. Season with pepper, salt (if required).

CHEESY LEEKS

8 medium leeks
1 1/2 oz (38g) butter
1 1/2 oz (38g) flour
1/2 pint (300ml) milk
6 oz (175g) Cheddar cheese, grated
1 teaspoon made mustard
SERVES 6

Trim and wash leeks well. Cook in boiling salted water until tender and drain, keeping about a quarter of the stock. Put in ovenproof dish. Melt butter and add flour, cook one minute then gradually stir in milk and leek stock. Continue stirring until sauce bubbles and thickens. Stir in 4 oz (125g) cheese and mustard and season. Pour over leeks, sprinkle over the rest of the cheese and grill to golden brown.

CHATEAU POTATOES

1 1/2 lb (675g) small new potatoes
2 oz (50g) butter
Seasoning
Chopped parsley or chives
SERVES 6

Scrape potatoes, melt the butter in a heavy pan and add potatoes. Cover and cook gently, shaking occasionally until cooked and golden brown. Season and garnish with parsley and chives.

CREAMED CABBAGE

2 oz (50g) butter
1 lb (450g) cabbage,
coarsely chopped
Salt and pepper
¼ teaspoon grated nutmeg
3 fl oz (80ml) double
cream
SERVES 4-6

Melt the butter in a heavy frying pan and add the cabbage. Fry gently, stirring frequently for about 10 minutes, until it is softened but crunchy. Season with salt, pepper and nutmeg then stir in cream and cook 3-5 minutes.

CREAMED PARSNIPS

1 lb (450g) parsnips
½ level teaspoon salt
Sauce
1 oz (25g) plain flour
4 fl oz (125ml) milk
Salt and pepper
1 teaspoon grated orange
rind
SERVES 4-6

Peel parsnips and quarter lengthways, simmer until tender, drain well and keep about a quarter of a pint of liquid. Put the flour into a small saucepan, blend in milk and cooking liquid and seasoning. When thickened stir in the orange rind and parsnips and heat through.

ONIONS IN CREAM SAUCE

1 lb (450g) small onions
½ pint (300ml) chicken
stock
½ pint (300ml) béchamel
sauce
¼ pint (150ml) single
cream
Pinch red pepper to garnish
Salt and pepper
SERVES 4-6

Skin onions and simmer in chicken stock for about 10 minutes. Drain well and cool slightly. Stir cream into sauce and add onions, season to taste. Reheat gently.

PEASE PUDDING

1 lb (450g) dried split
peas
2 oz (50g) butter
1 egg, beaten
2 tablespoons chopped mint
(or 1 tablespoon dried
mint)
Salt and pepper
SERVES 4-6

Soak peas in cold water overnight. Drain, cover with fresh cold water in saucepan and simmer for 1 hour. Drain well and liquidise or sieve. Mix in other ingredients and season. Grease an ovenproof dish and put in the mixture, cover and bake for 30 minutes at Gas Mark 4, 350F, 180C.

POTATO BALLS WITH CHEESE

½ lb (225g) mashed potato
1 tablespoon grated
parmesan cheese
1 teaspoon parsley, chopped
finely
1 medium onion, chopped
finely
2 egg yolks
Breadcrumbs
Oil for frying
SERVES 2

Mix together all the ingredients but the breadcrumbs, make into walnut sized balls, roll in breadcrumbs and deep fry in oil.

ZUCCHINI SLICE

375g Zucchini (courgettes)
1 large onion
3 rashers bacon
1 cup (300ml) grated
Cheddar cheese
1 cup (300ml) self raising
flour
half a cup (150ml) oil
5 eggs
Salt and pepper

Grate unpeeled zucchini coarsely, finely chop onion and bacon. Combine zucchini, bacon, sifted flour, oil and lightly beaten egg, season with salt and pepper. Pour into well greased tin approximately 16x26cm. Cook for 30-40 minutes until brown. Oven Gas Mark 6, 400F, 200C.

FARMHOUSE WINTER VEGETABLE PIE

Filling

2 medium onions, peeled
3 large carrots, peeled
1 large parsnips, peeled
1 large leek, washed and trimmed
2 sticks celery, washed
1 pint (600ml) milk
1 bouquet garni
1 bay leaf

Pastry

8 oz (225g) plain flour
2 oz (50g) butter
2 oz (50g) lard
Pinch of salt
4 oz (115g) Cheddar cheese, finely grated
Cold Water

Sauce

1½ oz (37g) plain flour
1½ oz (37g) butter
Salt and pepper
Beaten egg for glazing
Milk is used from list above after cooking vegetables

SERVES 4-6

Roughly chop the vegetables. Place the onions, carrots and parsnips in a pan with the milk, bouquet garni and bay leaf. Bring to the boil and simmer until the vegetables are almost cooked, then add the leek and celery and cook for a further few minutes until all the vegetables are just tender. Meanwhile make up the pastry in the usual way, rubbing the fats into the flour to obtain a light crumb like mixture, adding the grated cheese before stirring in a little cold water to bind the pastry ingredients together. Roll out to fit the top of a 1 litre (2 pint) pie dish.

Strain the vegetables, reserve the milk but discard the bay leaf and the bouquet garni. Make the milk up to 1 pint (600ml) with a little extra milk as necessary. In a clean pan melt the remaining butter. Add the flour and cook for a few minutes, then add the milk gradually, mixing well. Heat, stirring constantly, until the sauce boils and thickens. Stir the vegetables into the sauce and add seasoning. Place vegetables and sauce in a pie dish, top with pastry and seal well. Brush with beaten egg and bake in a preheated oven at Gas Mark 5, 375F, 190C. for 20-25 minutes until the pastry is cooked and golden brown.

VEGETARIAN DISH

Selection of any vegetables
e.g. carrots, parsnips,
potatoes, peas, cabbage,
onions, broccoli.
4 oz (100g) mushrooms
1 cup wholemeal
breadcrumbs
½ pint (300ml) vegetable
stock
1 teaspoon mixed herbs

Partly cook the vegetables, chop into pieces and place in layers in large ovenproof dish. Sprinkle mixed herbs between each layer. Finally slice the mushrooms and place on top of the vegetables. Sprinkle with breadcrumbs and pour over the vegetable stock. Bake in a moderate oven for 20 minutes until piping hot. Salt not needed with herbs and stock.

MILD VEGETABLE CURRY

1 tablespoon (15ml) oil
1 onion, chopped
1 clove garlic, crushed
1 teaspoon (5ml) curry
powder
8 oz (225g) carrots, sliced
8 oz (225g) courgettes,
sliced
1 lb (450g) potatoes, diced
2 oz (50g) red lentils
1 tablespoon (15ml)
tomato puree
¾ pint (425ml) vegetable
stock
1 tablespoon (15ml)
mango chutney
½ teaspoon (2.5ml)
turmeric
Salt and pepper
SERVES 4-6

Heat oil in a large saucepan and lightly fry onion, garlic and curry powder for 2 minutes. Add remaining vegetables and lentils and stir in puree, stock, chutney and turmeric. Season well and bring to the boil. Cover and simmer for 15 minutes, stirring occasionally until tender. Cook for 15 minutes on top of oven, then 1 hour 15 minutes in the oven at Gas Mark 5, 375F, 190C. Serve with garlic bread or crusty rolls.

CELEBRATION ROLL

1 tablespoon (15ml) oil
1 large onion, chopped
1 clove garlic, chopped
3 sticks celery, finely chopped
6 oz (175g) fresh wholemeal breadcrumbs
2 oz (50g) pistachio nuts, chopped
2 oz (50g) no need to soak apricots, chopped
Salt and pepper
1 tablespoon (15ml) sage, chopped
1 egg, beaten
8 oz (225g) curd cheese
½ teaspoon nutmeg
1 lb (450g) whole leaf spinach, cooked
13 oz (375g) puff pastry
Beaten egg to glaze
SERVES 4

Heat oil and fry onion, garlic and celery for 5 minutes. Remove from heat and stir in breadcrumbs, nuts, sage, apricots, seasoning and egg to bind. Cool. Mix curd cheese with nutmeg. Squeeze out excess water from spinach. Roll out pastry 14x12 inch trim edges. Place half stuffing down middle lengthways. Arrange half the spinach to cover stuffing, then spread curd cheese over. Repeat with remaining spinach and stuffing. Dampen pastry edges and bring up over filling. Overlap edges to seal, then place roll, seam side down on a slightly oiled baking sheet. Brush with beaten egg. Decorate with pastry trimming and brush with egg again. Cook for 15-20 minutes until golden at Gas Mark 7, 425F, 220C. Freezes well — thaw for 2-3 hours and heat in hot oven for 15 minutes.

CHEESE SOUFFLÉ

¾ lb (300g) potatoes
2 oz (50ml) milk
½ oz (12.5 g) margarine
4 oz (100g) Cheddar cheese
2 eggs
Salt and pepper
SERVES 4

Grease an 8 inch soufflé dish. Peel, boil and mash potatoes. Add milk and margarine to mashed potatoes, stir over a low heat. Add grated cheese and stir until melted. Remove from heat. Season. Separate the yolks from egg whites and whisk these until stiff and forms peaks. Stir egg yolks into potato mixture, fold in the egg whites lightly. Pour into greased soufflé dish and bake in a hot oven until risen and brown. Cook for 20 minutes at Gas Mark 6, 400F, 200C.

CHEESE PIE

6 oz (150g) breadcrumbs
2 oz (50g) margarine
¾ pint (425g) milk
6 oz (150g) grated cheese
2 eggs
Salt and pepper
Pinch dry mustard
SERVES 4

Heat margarine and milk in pan, do not boil. Add breadcrumbs, cheese and seasoning. Stir in egg yolks. Whisk egg whites until stiff and gently fold into mixture. Put in greased pie dish. Bake in oven for 30 minutes at 350F, 180C, Gas 4, then turn down to Gas Mark 3, 325F. and cook for a further 20 minutes.

YORKSHIRE SAVOURY

¾ lb (350g) potatoes
1 small onion
4 oz (125g) grated cheese
½ teaspoon dried sage
4 oz (125g) plain flour
½ teaspoon (2.5ml) salt
¼ pint (142ml) milk
¼ pint (142ml) water
Knob of lard
SERVES 4

Peel and slice potatoes and onion. Put lard into small roasting tin then into oven to melt. Put half potatoes, half onions and one third of cheese in tin in layers. Sprinkle with sage, then repeat. Make up batter with remaining ingredients, then pour into roasting tin over the layers. Sprinkle with cheese. Cook for 40 minutes at Gas Mark 7, 425F, 220C.

BROCCOLI PUFF

8 oz (220g) broccoli
1 tin (295g) cream of
mushroom soup
4 oz (100g) sharp
Cheddar cheese, grated
2 fl oz (60ml) milk
2 fl oz (60ml) mayonnaise
2 oz (50g) Ritz cracker
crumbs
1 egg, beaten
Butter
SERVES 4

Cook broccoli, drain and chop. Place in bottom of 10x6 inch (25x15cm) baking dish. Mix soup and cheese. Add milk, mayonnaise and beaten egg to soup mixture. Pour over broccoli. Sprinkle crumbs on top and dot with butter. Bake at Gas Mark 4, 350F, 185C. for 45 minutes, uncovered.

ONION AND EGG GOUGERE

Choux Pastry
½ pint (150ml) water
2 oz (50g) butter or
margarine
2½ oz (65g) flour
2 eggs
Pinch of salt
Filling
6 hard boiled eggs, peeled
2 oz (50g) Cheddar cheese
1 bunch spring onions,
chopped
4 oz (100g) chopped
mushrooms
½ pint (300ml) milk
1 oz (25g) butter
1 oz (25g) flour
Salt and pepper
Sprig of thyme, parsley and
a bay leaf
SERVES 4

Melt the margarine in water in a pan. Bring to the boil. Add sieved flour all at once and beat really hard until smooth. Beating well between each application, add beaten eggs gradually. Pipe or spoon round edges of a 9 inch flan dish. Add herbs to the milk and bring to the boil, cover and leave to infuse. Melt margarine in a pan add flour and cook for 1 minute. Strain the milk, add gradually stirring all the time, bring to the boil. Grate cheese and add with remaining ingredients to taste. Chop the eggs in half; arrange in centre of dish, cover the eggs with the filling. Cook for 40 minutes at Gas Mark 6, 400F, 200C.

CHEESE, ONION AND EGG BAKE

1 large onion, finely sliced
4-6 oz (100-150g) grated
hard cheese
2 eggs
A little margarine, about 1
oz (25g)
SERVES 2

Heat the margarine in a pan, add the onions, keeping them stirred. Cook until tender without browning. Put in the bottom of an ovenproof dish. Cover with two-thirds of the cheese. Make two slight depressions, break the eggs carefully into these. Cover with the remaining cheese. Cover with a lid and bake at Gas Mark 5, 375F, 190C. for15-20 minutes, until the egg white is set. Serve with a green salad and jacket potatoes or arrange a circle of sliced tomatoes and mushrooms on top before baking; or some rings of sliced blanched pepper.

VEGETABLE LASAGNE

8 oz (225g) carrots, peeled
and thinly sliced
8 oz (225g) courgettes,
trimmed and thinly sliced
1 onion, skinned and
thinly sliced
4 oz (100g) celery, cleaned
and thinly sliced
1 chicken stock cube
1 oz (25g) butter
2 level teaspoons (10ml)
flour
½ pint (300ml) milk
6 oz (175g) ready to use
lasagne
6 oz (175g) mature
cheddar, grated
Salt and black pepper
SERVES 4

Place vegetables in a pan with the stock cube and half a pint of boiling water. Bring to the boil and cover and simmer for 10 minutes. Melt butter in a pan, stir in flour. Cook gently for 1 minute. Remove from heat and stir in the milk. Cook until sauce thickens. If sauce is too thick add liquid from vegetables. Make alternate layers of lasagne, cheese and vegetables, using only 4 oz cheese, finishing with a layer of lasagne. Pour over sauce then sprinkle with remaining cheese. Bake in oven for 30 minutes at Gas Mark 5, 375F, 190C.

MUSHROOM AND BEAN MEDLEY

1 large onion
4 celery sticks
12 oz (300g) mushrooms
2 oz (50g) butter or
margarine
1 tablespoon wholemeal flour
¼ pint (150ml) vegetable stock
½ teaspoon thyme
Bay leaf
1 tin (294g) flageolet beans
¼ pint (150ml) yoghurt
Seasoning to taste
Chopped parsley to garnish
SERVES 4

Slice mushrooms, onion and celery. Melt butter in a saucepan and fry onions and celery until onion is transparent. Add mushrooms and stir occasionally over medium heat for 2-3 minutes. Sift in flour, then add stock and herbs. Bring to boil, add flageolet beans and continue to cook for 2-3 minutes. Take off the heat and stir in the natural yoghurt. Heat through very gently to prevent curdling. Serve on a bed of rice with a tossed green salad.

BROAD BEAN PIE

2 lb (1 kilo) shelled broad
beans
1 large onion, chopped
½ teaspoon dried sage
¼ pint (150ml) water
½ teaspoon yeast extract
(Marmite)
3 tablespoons wholemeal
flour
2 tablespoons skimmed
milk
2 eggs, beaten
1 oz (25g) cheese, grated
2 oz (50g) fresh wholemeal
breadcrumbs
SERVES 6

Cook beans, sage and onion in water. Drain before beans are fully cooked and save liquid. Mix Marmite to cooking liquid to make a stock. Place cooked vegetables into a greased ovenproof dish and pour over the stock. Mix flour with milk until smooth. Then stir in eggs and cheese. Spread over the vegetables, sprinkle with breadcrumbs and bake at Gas Mark 4, 350F, 180C for 30 minutes or until brown.

LENTIL PIE

4 oz (100g) pre-
soaked/washed red lentils
4 oz (100g) peeled and
sliced potatoes
1 large onion, chopped
1 large carrot, chopped
1½ pints (900ml)
vegetable stock (use cube)
1 tablespoon Worcestershire
sauce
½ teaspoon mixed herbs
4 oz (100g) wholewheat
macaroni
2 oz (50g) cheese, grated
Seasoning
SERVES 4-6

Boil potatoes, carrots, onion until almost cooked. Put the pre-washed lentils to stock, Worcestershire sauce, herbs and seasoning. Simmer in covered pan for 30 minutes. Add the pre-cooked vegetables (more stock may be required) and cook for a further 30 minutes until vegetables are tender. Liquidise or mash the mixture. Cook macaroni in boiling water until just tender, drain and add to the lentil mixture in pan and reheat. Turn into an ovenproof dish, sprinkle with cheese and brown under the grill.

VEGETABLE FRICASSÉE

12 oz (300g) swede
8 oz (200g) potato
8 oz (200g) carrots
1 large leek
half a small cauliflower
¾ pint (450ml) vegetable
stock or water
2 oz (50g)
polyunsaturated margarine
2 oz (50g) wholemeal
flour
Skimmed milk
1 teaspoon lemon juice
Seasoning
Chopped parsley
SERVES 4-6

Cut vegetables into ¾ inch (2cm) chunks. Break cauliflower into florets. Bring stock to the boil in saucepan, add swede and carrots. Return to boil, add potatoes and simmer for 5 minutes. Add leeks and cauliflower and cook for a further 3-5 minutes until vegetables are tender but still crisp. Drain, reserving stock. Keep the vegetables warm. Melt margarine in a saucepan, stir in flour and cook for 1 minute. Make stock up to ¾ pint (450ml) with skimmed milk and add to saucepan stirring and bring to boil. Reduce heat, add remaining ingredients and simmer for 2-3 minutes. Pour sauce over vegetables and serve at once with rice. This recipe can also be served in individual ovenproof dishes topped with grated Edam cheese and wholemeal breadcrumbs and browned under the grill. Alternatively use as a pie filling or pancake stuffing.

VEGETABLE SAVOURY

1 lb 8 oz (1kg) mixed
vegetables (fresh, frozen or
tinned, well-drained)
2 eggs, well beaten
7 oz (225g) tin tomatoes
(chopped)
4 oz (100g) mature
Cheddar cheese, sliced
1 tomato sliced
4 slices wholemeal toast,
buttered.
SERVES 2-4

Put the vegetables in a 3 pint (2 litre) bowl. Season well and stir in the eggs and tomatoes. Cover with cling film and cook in the microwave oven (650 watt) on HIGH for 2 minutes, then uncover and cook for a further 2 minutes. Arrange the cheese slices over the top followed by the tomato slices. Cook uncovered on HIGH for 2 minutes. Divide the mixture evenly to the wholemeal toast and serve at once. If a microwave oven is not available, cook the mixture for 15-20 minutes in the first instance, then after adding the cheese and tomato cook for another 5-10 minutes.

Chapter Eight

Salads, Sauces and Stuffings

TOMATO AND KIWI

6 medium tomatoes
2 Kiwi fruit
4 tablespoons (60ml)
French dressing
Parsley, to garnish

Thinly slice tomatoes and place on a flat dish overlapping. Thinly peel Kiwi and slice. Arrange on top of tomatoes. Coat with a well seasoned French dressing. Garnish with parsley.

CHEESE AND ORANGE

8 oz (225g) Edam cheese
2 oranges
Small carton yoghurt
2 tablespoons (30ml)
lemon juice
1 bunch watercress

Cube cheese. Peel and segment orange. Strip watercress. Mix together then stir lemon juice into yoghurt and pour over salad. Stir everything together.

GRAPEFRUIT AND PEPPER

2 grapefruits
1 small green pepper
8 oz (200g) cooked potato
1 medium onion
1 tablespoon (15ml) salad oil
1 dessertspoon (10ml)
wine vinegar
Salt and pepper to taste

Peel grapefruit and divide into segments by cutting out flesh in between membranes. Cut green pepper into thin strips and cut potato into small dice. Slice onion and separate slices into rings. Place these into a bowl adding oil, vinegar and seasoning to taste. Toss lightly together. Refrigerate 30 minutes before serving. Good with poultry and liver.

VINAIGRETTE DRESSING

3 tablespoons oil
Add 1-2 tablespoons vinegar
$\frac{1}{4}$ teaspoon salt
$\frac{1}{4}$ teaspoon mustard
$\frac{1}{4}$ teaspoon sugar and pepper

Shake all together in a screw topped jar. As an alternative to the vinegar use white, tarragon or garlic vinegar

RUSSIAN SALAD

half a medium lettuce
8 oz (200g) cold cooked
potato
8 oz (200g) cold cooked
carrots
6 oz (150g) cold cooked peas
6 oz (150g) green beans,
cooked and sliced
1 tablespoon (15ml) chopped
capers or gherkins
Mayonnaise
2 hard boiled eggs, sliced

Line serving dish with the lettuce. Dice potatoes and carrots. Put into bowl with peas, beans and capers or gherkins. Toss with sufficient mayonnaise to coat thoroughly. Heap on top of lettuce and garnish with egg slices.

CREAM CHEESE AND CARROT

2 medium carrots
2 oz (50g) sultanas or raisins
1 carton cottage cheese (or
Philadelphia)
2 oz (50g) chopped walnuts
¼ pint mayonnaise
Salt and pepper
2 oz (50g) Cheddar cheese
A little Worcester sauce

Grate carrot, add sultanas, walnuts and cheddar cheese. Season, mix in cottage cheese (or Philadelphia) and mayonnaise. Serve as an accompaniment to any meat dish. Good for freezing (Storage time 2-3 weeks).

GOLDEN APPLE SALAD

1 lb (450g) yellow apples
washed and cored
Juice of half a lemon
3 oz (75g) shelled walnuts
4 oz (125g) stoned dates,
quartered
3½ fl oz (112ml) double
cream whipped to peaks
3½ fl oz (112ml)
mayonnaise
Lettuce leaves
1 tablespoon marmalade.

Cut, (do not peel) apples into large dice. Place in a bowl, sprinkle with lemon juice. Add dates and nuts and toss. In separate bowl blend mayonnaise and cream, then fold in marmalade. Add to apple mixture and mix well. Turn onto platter lined with lettuce leaves, garnish with grated orange rind. Chill for several hours. Good with cold duck or goose.

MINTED POTATO

1 lb (450g) new potatoes
1 head lettuce, washed and
dried
1 tablespoon finely chopped
mint leaves
1 tablespoon vinegar
1 level tablespoon caster
sugar
1 hard boiled egg

Boil potatoes in skins until tender, skin quickly and cut into neat slices whilst hot. Put mint, sugar and vinegar in a small bowl and allow to stand at least an hour. Line a salad bowl with lettuce leaves, place potato slices in layers, sprinkling mint, sugar and vinegar over each layer. Decorate with hard boiled egg.

SUNSHINE SALAD

2 oz (50g) raisins
4 oz (125g) salted peanuts
2 oranges in segments
2 carrots, grated
Salad cream
1 tablespoon lemon juice
Lettuce, cress and tomato

Mix the raisins, peanuts, orange and carrot together add lemon juice and salad cream. Serve on a bed of lettuce, garnish with cress and tomato.

SWEETCORN SALAD

1 small tin corn
1 small tin pineapple rings
1 small packet frozen peas
Chopped parsley (optional)
4 sweet red-skinned apples
1 oz (25g) sultanas

Drain and cut pineapple into small pieces. Cut apple into small pieces leaving red skin on. Cook and drain peas, chop celery if used. Put all into a bowl and mix well, stir in mayonnaise to taste just before serving. Serves 8. Will freeze with mayonnaise.

WINTER SALAD

$\frac{1}{4}$ white cabbage
2 carrots
2 celery stalks
1 Cox's apple
1 orange
Salad cream
Sugar
Seasoning
4 oz (125g) dates

Finely slice cabbage and celery, grate carrot. Cut up dates and apple, segment the orange. Mix all together with salad cream, adding a little sugar and/or a squeeze of lemon juice if desired.

SALAD CREAM

1 oz (25g) flour
1 oz (25g) melted margarine
1 level dessertspoon mustard
2 eggs
1 level dessertspoon sugar
$\frac{1}{2}$ level dessertspoon salt
$\frac{1}{4}$ pint (150ml) milk
4 to 6 dessertspoons vinegar

Place in a basin the dry ingredients, work out any lumps. Mix with the melted margarine. Blend well the egg and milk, add to dry ingredients, add vinegar carefully. Cook until thick, put into sterilised bottles and seal (This salad dressing keeps well).

WHITE SAUCE – POURING

½ oz (13g) butter
½ oz (13g) flour
½ pint (300ml) milk
pepper and salt.

Basic recipe for 'roux' method.

Melt the butter in a saucepan, draw pan to the side of heat. Add flour and mix well with wooden spoon. Add about one third of the milk, stir carefully, return to heat until bubbling, add the rest of the milk gradually, bring to the boil for 3 minutes. Season. This sauce forms the foundation for other sauces.

WHITE SAUCE – COATING

As above using 1 oz (25g) margarine or butter, 1 oz (25g) flour, half a pint (300ml) of milk.

VARIATIONS:

Anchovy | Add 1 teaspoon essence of anchovy to each 1 pint (600ml) white sauce.

Caper | Add 1 dessertspoon capers and a little of the caper vinegar to each half pint (300ml) white sauce.

Cheese | Add 1 oz (25g) grated cheese and 1 teaspoon made mustard to each half pint (300ml) white sauce.

Egg | Add 1 hard boiled egg, roughly chopped to each half pint (300ml) white sauce.

Mustard | Mix 1 teaspoon mustard with a dessertspoon vinegar, and add to each half pint (300ml) white sauce.

Onion | Add a large cooked onion, chopped very finely to each half pint (300ml) white sauce.

Parsley | Add 1 tablespoon finely chopped parsley to each half pint (300ml) white sauce.

Shrimp | Add 2 tablespoons shelled shrimps to each half pint (300ml) white sauce.

HOLLANDAISE SAUCE

3 tablespoons wine vinegar
Bay leaf
4 peppercorns
2 egg yolks
Seasoning
4 oz unsalted butter

Put vinegar, peppercorns and bay leaf in a pan and heat to reduce to one tablespoon. Cool. Put yolks in food processor, heat butter until bubbling, strain the vinegar and add to yolks, process. Whilst butter is still bubbling, pour in slow steady stream with machine going. Should thicken slightly, serve immediately.

BÉCHAMEL SAUCE

half an onion
1 stalk celery
1 sprig thyme
half a bay leaf
6 peppercorns
17 fl oz (500ml) milk
2 oz (50g) butter
2 tablespoons flour
Salt
Grated nutmeg

Place the onion, celery, herbs and peppercorns in the milk and bring to the boil. Set aside for 30 minutes. Melt the butter, add the flour and cook for 1 minute. Strain the milk and gradually add to the roux, stirring all the time. Bring to the boil, add the salt and a little grated nutmeg. Simmer for 2-3 minutes and season to taste.

TARTARE SAUCE

¼ pint (150ml) mayonnaise
1 teaspoon chopped capers
1 teaspoon chopped gherkin
1 teaspoon chopped parsley

Add the chopped gherkins, capers and parsley to the mayonnaise and serve cold.

MINT SAUCE

2 handfuls of fresh mint
(preferably apple mint)
Sugar to taste
¼ pint (150ml) Vinegar
2 tablespoons boiling water

Put mint in food processor, blend. Add sugar, blend, then add boiling water and blend. Finally blend the vinegar. Can be frozen for use in the winter.

SAGE AND ONION STUFFING

6 tablespoons breadcrumbs
1 dessertspoon chopped sage
Dash of pepper
½ teaspoon salt
3 large onions
2 oz (50g) butter

Boil the onions for 5 minutes. Add to the other ingredients after chopping finely. Add the melted fat and mix well.

FRUIT AND NUT STUFFING

2 oz (50g) no-soak prunes
2 oz (50g) dried apricots
4 tablespoons sherry
2 oz (50g) walnuts
coarsely chopped
2 oz (50g) almonds
1 oz (25g) butter
1 large onion, chopped
2 sticks celery, chopped
1 firm pear, chopped
1 Bramley apple, chopped
2 oz (50g) Kumquats
4 tablespoons chopped
parsley
1 teaspoon grated orange rind
1 teaspoon dried sage
½ teaspoon dried thyme
¼ teaspoon cinnamon
¼ teaspoon coriander
¼ teaspoon mace
Freshly ground black pepper
3 oz (75g) stale wholemeal
breadcrumbs
1 teaspoon Salt

This recipe is enough for a 10-12lb bird. Marinate the stoned prunes and quartered apricots in the wine overnight. Toast the nuts in the oven. Gently fry the celery and onion in butter for 2 minutes. Add the apple and pear and cook again for 2 minutes. Add the spices and herbs, and fry a little to bring out the flavour. Add the remaining ingredients and mix well. Kumquats should be seeded and chopped, with pips removed.

Chapter Nine

Hot Puddings

CHERRY ALMOND CLAFOUTIS

1 oz (25g) toasted flaked almonds
3 eggs
3 oz (75g) caster sugar
Few drops vanilla essence
2 tablespoons (30ml) Kirsch or cherry brandy
3 oz (75g) plain flour, sifted
9 fl oz (270ml) milk
16 oz (450g) fresh cherries
Icing sugar for dredging
SERVES 4

Grease a one litre (2 pint) ovenproof dish and sprinkle with almonds. Whisk eggs, caster sugar and vanilla essence together until thick and creamy. Fold in Kirsch or cherry brandy then the flour. Slowly beat in milk until mixture is smooth. Pour into dish and arrange cherries on top. Bake 40-45 minutes in oven Gas Mark 4, 350F, 180C. until light and golden. Serve dredged with icing sugar and whipped cream.

NEW ENGLAND APPLE CAKE

3 oz (75g) pecans or any available nut
12 oz (350g) cooking apple
4 oz (125g) butter
7 oz (200g) granulated sugar
1 egg
1 teaspoon baking powder
½ teaspoon (2.5ml) salt
1 teaspoon (5ml) cinnamon
1 teaspoon (5ml) nutmeg
5 oz (150g) self raising flour
Caramel Sauce (optional)
4 oz (125g) butter
7 oz (200g) light brown sugar
½ teaspoon (2.5ml) salt
1 teaspoon (5ml) vanilla extract
4 fl oz (150ml) evaporated milk
SERVES 8-10

Preheat oven Gas Mark 4, 350F, 180C. Grind or chop nuts and finely peel and slice apple to about the size of almonds. Cream butter (which should be at room temperature) and sugar, add egg until blended. Add baking powder, salt, cinnamon and nutmeg and mix well together. Add flour, apples and nuts. Pour mixture into a greased 9" round cake tin and bake for 30 minutes or until the top springs back when touched. Cool slightly — centre may sink slightly. Garnish with whipped cream and slices of unpeeled apple. May be served also with ice cream or the Caramel sauce.

For Sauce melt butter, brown sugar and salt in small saucepan over a medium heat. Stir in vanilla and evaporated milk. Bring to the boil stirring with a whisk. This sauce can be made ahead of time and reheated over hot water. A refrigerated cake will keep for a week.

BREAD AND BUTTER PUDDING

1 ½ oz (40g) butter
4 slices white bread
(remove crusts)
4 tablespoons (60ml)
apricot jam or marmalade
1 oz (25g) cut mixed peel
(optional)
1 oz (25g) sultanas
¾ pint (425ml) milk
2 tablespoons (30ml)
sugar
2 eggs beaten
SERVES 4

Use ½ oz butter to grease a 2 pint ovenproof dish. Butter bread and spread with jam cut into small triangles. Layer bread in dish, sprinkle with peel and sultanas between layers. Heat milk and sugar to just below boiling. Whisk in eggs then strain over bread and butter. Leave to soak for 30 minutes. Place dish in a roasting tin with water to halfway up dish. Bake in preheated oven for 45 minutes, then increase heat and cook for a further 10-15 minutes until crisp and golden on top and set. Serve at once. Gas Mark 4, 350F, 180C, then Gas Mark 5, 375F, 190C.

HOT SWISS TRIFLE

½ Swiss roll (or whole
small one)
1 small (415g) tin fruit
cocktail
2 level tablespoons
(2x15ml) custard powder
2 eggs, separated
4 tablespoons (4x15ml)
sugar
¾ pint (450ml) milk

Heat oven Gas Mark 3, 325F, 170C and prepare 1 ½ pint pie dish. Slice Swiss roll thinly and use to line pie dish. Cover with drained fruit. Mix custard powder, egg yolks and 1 tablespoon sugar to smooth cream with little milk and put rest of milk on to boil. When nearly boiling, pour onto mixed custard powder, stirring well. Return custard to pan and boil, stirring all the time. Pour over fruit. Whisk egg whites until stiff. Gradually whisk in 2 level tablespoons sugar for each egg white. Cover trifle with meringue, dust with sugar and bake for 10-15 minutes.

STICKY BUTTERSCOTCH PUDDING

6 oz (175g) cooking dates, apricots or raisins
½ teaspoon (2.5ml) bicarbonate of soda
½ pint (284ml) boiling water
3 oz (75g) soft margarine
5 oz (150g) soft brown sugar
1 egg beaten
1 teaspoon (5ml) pure vanilla
8 oz (225g) self raising white or brown flour
1 teaspoon (5ml) baking powder
Sauce
3 oz (75g) butter
5 oz (150g) soft brown sugar
¼ pint (142ml) double or whipping cream

Cut up dates or apricots into small pieces. Sprinkle on bicarbonate. Pour on water and leave to soak and cool. Cream together margarine and sugar until pale and fluffy. Beat in the eggs and vanilla. Sieve together flour and baking powder and fold in with the fruit mixture. Place in a well greased 2 pint (1200ml) basin. Cook for about 40 minutes at Gas Mark 4, 350F, 180C.

For sauce place all ingredients in saucepan stir and bring to the boil, simmer for about 3 minutes. The pudding is served hot turned out onto a serving dish and the sauce poured over it. You could also serve with vanilla ice-cream.

APRICOT LAYER PUDDING

3 oz (75g) soft margarine
3 oz (75g) caster sugar
1 large egg
4 oz (125g) self raising
flour
1 level teaspoon (5ml)
baking powder
2 dessertspoons (25ml)
milk
Tin apricots
Sauce
1 level tablespoon (15ml)
custard powder
Apricot juice
SERVES 4

Grease deep oven dish. Place all cake ingredients into a large bowl and mix well together adding slightly more milk if required to make a dropping consistency. Drain apricots, reserving juice, arrange half of fruit in dish, cover with half mixture. Smooth and repeat with remaining ingredients. Bake in centre of oven for 40 minutes approximately at Gas Mark 4, 350F, 180C. Serve with Apricot Sauce. Make up juice to half a pint — blend in custard powder, bring to boil and stirring cook for 1 minute.

SOURED CREAM APPLE CAKE

1 tablespoon (15ml)
demerara sugar
2 (175/225g) Granny
Smith apples
4 oz (100g) caster sugar
2 eggs, separated
4 oz (100g) self raising
flour
5 fl oz (150ml) soured
cream or 5 fl oz (150ml)
plain yoghurt
2-3 drops almond essence
1 oz (25g) chopped
almonds
SERVES 4

Line base of 8 inch (20cm) sandwich tin with baking parchment. Sprinkle with the demerara sugar. Arrange the apples slices to cover. Cream butter and sugar. Beat in the egg yolks and flour. Fold in almonds, soured cream (or yoghurt) and almond essence. Whisk egg whites until stiff and fold into cake mixture and then pour it over the apples. Cook for 45 minutes to 1 hour at Gas Mark 4, 350F, 180C. Turn out of tin, apples uppermost. Serve warm with cream.

QUICK APPLE STRUDEL

*Small packet frozen puff
pastry
½ oz (14g) butter
Filling (mixed together)
1 lb (450g) cooking apples
2 oz (50g) sugar
2 oz (50g) sultanas
1 teaspoon (5ml)
cinnamon
SERVES 4*

Roll out pastry paper thin approximately 21 inch square. Spread filling over two thirds of pastry and roll up from apple end. Place in baking tray, horseshoe shape. Melt butter and brush top of strudel. Bake in hot oven Gas Mark 6, 400F, 200C for about 30 minutes. Serve hot sprinkled with sugar — will make 8 individual strudels.

PINEAPPLE SPONGE CUSTARD

*8 oz (225g) slices canned
pineapple with 4
tablespoons (60ml) syrup
2 tablespoons (30ml) self
raising flour
2 teaspoons (10ml) caster
sugar
Juice and grated zest of 1
lemon
2 eggs, separated
¼ pint (142ml) skimmed
milk
SERVES 4*

Reserve 1 slice of pineapple. Chop the remainder into half-inch pieces. Arrange the chopped pineapple in a 2 pint soufflé dish. In a large bowl combine the flour and sugar. Mix together the lemon juice, syrup and egg yolks. Gradually beat into the flour and sugar to form a thin batter. Whisk egg whites until peaking, carefully fold into the batter. Gently pour the batter over the chopped pineapple, place the soufflé dish in a baking tin containing 1 inch hot water. Bake for 55 minutes or until golden brown and firm to touch. Decorate with reserved slice of pineapple and serve immediately. Gas Mark 4, 350F, 180C.

RASPBERRY LATTICE DESSERT

4 oz (125g) plain flour
2 oz (50g) caster sugar
½ teaspoon (2.5ml) baking powder
½ teaspoon (2.5ml) ground cinnamon
2 oz (50g) ground almonds
2 oz (50g) ground rice
Grated rind of one lemon
4 oz (125g) butter
2-3 tablespoons (30-40ml) milk
3-4 tablespoons (60ml) raspberry jam
1 beaten egg
Icing sugar for dusting
SERVES 6

To the sieved flour add sugar, baking powder, cinnamon, ground almonds, ground rice, and lemon rind. Rub in butter. Add milk to make firm dough. Knead well. Leave in fridge for 30 minutes. Roll out two-thirds of the pastry and press into 8 inch (20cm) flan ring. Spread jam on the top. Roll out the remaining pastry and cut into strips, arrange in a lattice pattern on top, press down lightly. Glaze pastry with beaten egg. Bake for 30-40 minutes at Gas Mark 5, 375F, 190C. Cool then remove flan ring, and dust with icing sugar.

BORDER TART

6 oz shortcrust pastry
4 oz (100g) margarine
4 oz (100g) caster sugar
2 oz (50g) ground almonds
4 oz (100g) currants
2 beaten eggs
Almond essence
SERVES 6

Line a 8 inch (20cm) flan dish with short pastry. Cream margarine and sugar, add eggs and all other ingredients. Pour into uncooked pastry case and bake at 325-375F for 30 minutes or until golden brown and set. Dust with icing sugar and serve with cream.

RHUBARB AND ORANGE TART

8 oz (225g) shortcrust
pastry
1 lb (450g) rhubarb
6 oz (175g) sugar
1 oz (25g) flour
1 beaten egg
Grated rind of 1 orange
2 tablespoons of orange
juice make up with water
to $\frac{1}{4}$ pint (150ml)
8 inch (20cm) ovenproof
plate
SERVES 4

Make the shortcrust pastry, line the ovenproof plate saving the trimmings for the lattice. Wipe the rhubarb and cut into 1 inch lengths place on pastry case. In a basin blend together sugar, flour, eggs and rind of the orange. Place juice and water in a pan and bring to the boil. Pour onto flour mixture and stir briskly. Return to the pan and bring to the boil stirring all the time. Pour over the rhubarb, put strips from pastry trimmings on top to form a lattice. Cook at Gas Mark 6, 400F, 200C for 30 minutes. Serve hot or cold.

CHOCOLATE UP AND OVER PUDDING

4 oz (125g) soft
margarine
4 oz (125g) sugar
2 eggs
3 oz (75g) self raising
flour
1 oz (25g) cocoa
Topping and Sauce
1 rounded tablespoon cocoa
1 $\frac{1}{2}$ oz (38g) chopped nuts
(walnuts)
4 oz (125g) demerara
sugar
$\frac{1}{2}$ pint (250ml) hot,
strong black coffee

Grease deep ovenproof dish. Sieve flour and cocoa into bowl with other pudding ingredients (all in method). Mix well and beat 2 minutes until smooth. Put mixture into dish and smooth top. For topping and sauce, mix cocoa, nuts and 2 oz demerara sugar, sprinkle over pudding. Sweeten hot coffee with 2 oz sugar. Pour over pudding. Bake in moderate oven, Gas Mark 4, 350F, 180C for 50 minutes to 1 hour. During cooking it reverses, serve hot with cream or ice-cream.

CRUNCHY CHERRY PIE

6 oz (175g) plain flour
1½ oz (38g) margarine
1½ oz (38g) lard
1½ oz (38g) demerara sugar
1 14 oz (400g) tin cherry
pie filling
Cold water to mix
1½ oz (38g) chopped or
flaked almonds
SERVES 4-6

Rub fats into flour, remove approximately a third of dry mixture to another bowl, add sugar and almonds and mix together. Add sufficient water to two thirds mixture to make pastry. Line one 7 inch pie tin or flan dish. Spread pie filling over base, sprinkle almond and sugar mixture over top. Bake until cooked and lightly browned at Gas Mark 6, 400F, 200C for 25-30 minutes, serve with custard, cream or ice-cream.

CHOCOLATE SPONGE PUDDING

8 oz (225g) self raising
flour
Pinch of salt
½ oz (13g) cocoa
1 egg
3 oz (75g) margarine
3 oz (75g) sugar
3 tablespoons milk
Few drops vanilla essence
SERVES 6

Cream sugar and margarine together, break in egg, add dry ingredients and milk and the vanilla essence. Steam in greased covered basin for 1 hour 30 minutes.

ALTERNATIVE PUDDINGS

Jam	2 tablespoons in base of greased pudding basin
Treacle	2 tablespoons in base of greased pudding basin
Ginger	2 teaspoons ginger add with flour
Orange	Grated rind and juice add with flour
Lemon	Grated rind and juice add with flour
Fruit	2 oz (50g) mixed fruit add with flour

TO MICROWAVE PUDDINGS: Place in oven and cook for approximately 5 minutes or until ready on full power.

CHRISTMAS PUDDINGS

½ lb (250g) each of
currants, sultanas, raisins,
fine bread crumbs, suet and
demerara sugar
6 oz (175g) mixed
candied peel
4 oz (125g) flour
4 oz (125g) grated carrot
1 teaspoon mixed spice
1 teaspoon nutmeg
½ teaspoon cinnamon
1 teaspoon each vanilla
and almond essence
1 tablespoon golden syrup
Juice and finely grated rind
of 1 large lemon
4 eggs
¼ pint (150ml) milk
2 tablespoons brandy
SERVES 6-8

Mix dry ingredients together. Add syrup, lemon, flavourings, beaten egg, milk and brandy and mix thoroughly. Steam or boil for at least 6 hours. Will make approximately 2x100g and 1x500g pudding.

DANISH CHERRY PIE

14 oz (400g) tin cherry
pie filling
4 oz (125g) ground
almonds
6 oz (175g) icing sugar
2 eggs
SERVES 4

Using one of the flan pastries line a 8 inch flan ring. Cover flan base with pie filling. Mix ground almonds, icing sugar together, combine with the beaten eggs and beat mixture well, pour over filling. Bake for 45 minutes at Gas Mark 6, 400F, 200C.

RASPBERRY AND ALMOND TART

8 oz (225g) raspberries,
fresh or frozen
1 dessertspoon cornflour
2 egg whites
4 oz (125g) sugar
1 oz (25g) ground
almonds
Flaked almonds for
decoration
SERVES 4-6

Using one of the flan pastries line a 8 inch flan ring and bake blind. Combine the cornflour and raspberries gently, allow to stand and absorb juice. Transfer into flan case. Whisk egg whites, fold in sugar and ground almonds, place on top of filling and decorate with flaked almonds. Gently cook until the meringue is crisp in a moderate oven, Gas Mark 4, 350F, 180C. Serve with cream.

GROUND RICE MERINGUE

1 pint (600ml) milk
1 ½ oz (38g) ground rice
1 oz (25g) sugar
2 eggs
Pinch of salt
4 oz (125g) caster sugar
for meringue
SERVES 4

Mix the ground rice, 1 oz sugar and pinch of salt with a little milk. Boil the remainder and pour it on the rice, stirring. Return to pan, stir until it boils, cook for 5 minutes. Cool slightly. Separate the eggs, beat the yolks in rice mixture. Pour into greased pie dish, put in oven to form skin on top. Make meringues with the egg whites and 4 oz (125g) caster sugar, pile on top, crisp in oven at Gas Mark 1, 275F, 140C for 30 minutes to 1 hour.

LEMON LAYER PUDDING

Grated rind and juice of 2
small lemons
2 oz (50g) butter or
margarine
4 oz (125g) sugar
2 eggs separated
2 oz (50g) self raising
flour
½ pint (250ml) milk
SERVES 4

Add lemon rind to butter and sugar and beat until pale and fluffy. Add egg yolks and flour and beat well. Stir in milk and 2-3 tablespoons lemon juice. Whisk egg whites until stiff and fold in mixture, pour into buttered ovenproof dish. Stand in shallow tin of water and cook in oven Gas Mark 6, 400F, 200C for 45 minutes, until top is set and spongy to the touch. This pudding separates into a custard layer with a sponge top.

TREACLE CUSTARD TART

1 unbaked shortcrust pastry
flan case
4 tablespoons golden syrup
1 teaspoon finely grated
lemon rind
½ oz (13g) butter
2 tablespoons single cream
1 egg beaten
SERVES 4-6

Warm syrup and lemon rind, add butter and melt. Beat cream and egg together, blend into syrup. Pour into flan case. Bake in moderate oven 30-40 minutes until pastry is cooked and filling is set (Gas Mark 4, 350F, 180C). Serve hot or cold with cream if wished.

ORANGE MERINGUE PUDDING

1 tin rice pudding, family
sized or;
1 pint (600ml) home
made rice pudding
1 small tin mandarin
oranges
2 eggs
4 oz (125g) caster sugar
SERVES 4

Put rice pudding in ovenproof dish, separate eggs carefully and thoroughly. Stir yolks into rice mixture, followed by drained mandarin oranges. Make meringue with two egg whites and sugar. Pile on top of rice mixture, crisp in oven for 30-45 minutes at Gas Mark 1, 275F, 140C.

Chapter Ten

Cold Puddings

CHOCOLATE ROULADE WITH ORANGE CREAM

Sponge base
3 eggs size 3, separated
3 oz (75g) caster sugar
1 oz (25g) cocoa, sieved
Filling
5 oz (125ml) double cream
Grated rind of 1 orange
2 tablespoons (30ml) icing sugar
1 tablespoon (15ml) brandy
1 oz (25g) icing sugar for rolling
SERVES 6

For the roulade whisk egg yolks and sugar until thick. Fold in cocoa. Using clean beaters, whisk egg whites until stiff. Stir a spoonful into the chocolate mixture to slacken it. Carefully fold in the remaining egg white. Pour into a 7x11 inch Swiss roll tin, greased and lined and bake at Gas Mark 4, 350F, 180C for 15-20 minutes. Remove from oven and cover with a tea-towel and allow to cool completely.

For the filling whisk the cream until just starting to thicken. Add orange rind, 2 tablespoons icing sugar and brandy. Continue whisking until softly stiff. Turn the roulade out onto a sheet of greaseproof paper, liberally sprinkled with icing sugar. Spread with the cream and roll up loosely.

BANANA CARAMEL TART

1 small tin condensed milk
6 oz (150g) crushed digestive biscuits
2 oz (50g) butter
1 dessertspoon (10ml) syrup
2 small bananas
¼ pint (125ml) whipping cream
SERVES 4

Put tin condensed milk in pan of water and boil for three hours. Allow to cool. Melt butter and syrup gently in a pan. Remove pan from heat and stir in biscuit crumbs. Spread biscuit mix to the bottom and up the sides of a lined 8 inch cake tin and press to firm it. Leave in a cool place to harden. Put sliced bananas on biscuit base. Spread the caramelised condensed milk over bananas. Whip the cream and pipe over the top. Decorate with chocolate curls or grated chocolate. Condensed milk can be prepared a few days in advance. A quick, naughty but special cold sweet. Also nice made with a sweet pastry case.

PASSION PUDDING

9 oz (250g) wholemeal
flour
2 teaspoons (10ml)
cinnamon
½ teaspoon salt
1 teaspoon (approx.)
nutmeg, freshly grated
1 teaspoon bicarbonate of
soda
3 eggs, size 3
2 fl. oz (55ml) soured
cream
6 fl oz (175ml) sunflower
oil
2 teaspoons (10ml)
vanilla essence
6 oz (175g) soft brown
sugar
6 oz (175g) raw sugar,
Muscovado or Barbados
11 oz (300g) grated carrot
3 oz (75g) desiccated
coconut
Topping
4 oz (110g) full fat cream
cheese
1 oz (25g) unsalted butter
2 oz (50g) sifted icing
sugar
Juice of half a lemon
SERVES 8-10

Preheat oven to Gas Mark 2, 300F, 150C. Line one 8 inch round cake tin with greaseproof paper. Place the eggs, soured cream, oil and essence into a bowl, then sieve the two sugars into the bowl and beat well. Fold in the dry ingredients. Followed by the carrots and coconut. Mix well. Place mixture into prepared tin and bake on the centre shelf for 1½-2 hours. When cake is cool mix the topping ingredients together and spread thickly over the top. Serve in slices and pour over single cream.

ORANGE MERINGUE GATEAU

1½ oz (35g) soft
margarine
3 oz (75g) fine sugar
3 egg yolks
3 oz (75g) self raising
flour
½ teaspoon (2.5ml) baking
powder
3 tablespoons (3x15ml)
single cream
Grated rind of 1 orange
Meringue
3 egg whites
6 oz (175g) caster sugar
Chopped nuts, if liked
Filling
½ pint (300g) double cream
1 tin mandarin oranges or
use orange segments
1 tablespoon (15ml)
Grand Marnier or orange
juice
SERVES 6-8

Oven Gas Mark 3-4, 325F, 160C. Line 2x8 inch tins well with greaseproof (well greased). Mix together (cream) sugar and margarine. Add egg yolks. Sieve self raising flour and baking powder and fold into mixture. Add cream — divide equally between tins. Whisk egg whites until stiff, fold in sugar. Add meringue to base, (pipe for top layer) and add nuts if liked. Pour meringue on other base. Bake for 30-40 minutes. When cakes are cold sandwich together with whipped cream flavoured with Grand Marnier or orange juice and place orange segments in cream (Cakes will keep several days in tin before assembling).

CHOCOLATE PARFAIT

½ lb (225g) plain chocolate
15 oz (445g) tin chestnut
puree
2 tablespoons (30ml)
water
2 eggs
1 oz (25g) caster sugar
6 oz (175g) unsalted butter
1 tablespoon (15ml) sherry
SERVES 6

Melt chocolate in pan with water. Add puree. Add beaten yolks and sugar. Add beaten butter (and sherry). Fold in stiffly beaten whites. Leave to set.

ALMOND AND APRICOT MERINGUE

8 oz (225g) caster sugar
4 egg whites
2 oz (50g) flaked almonds (optional)
Filling
7 oz (200g) tinned apricots (pureed)
1 tablespoon (15ml) Cointreau
½ pint (284ml) double cream
Decoration
2 oz (50g) flaked almonds, toasted
Grated dark chocolate
Icing sugar
SERVES 10

Oven Gas Mark 2, 300F, 150-160C. Whisk egg whites to stiff peaks, beat in half of sugar. Fold in rest of sugar and almonds if used. Line two trays with foil and lightly oil and spread meringue onto 2x8 inch circles, level top of one and peak up top of the other. Cook for 50 minutes, leave to cool and dry out in oven if possible. Whilst meringues are cooking place the 2 oz flaked almonds onto dish and toast at the same time. Whip cream until thick, add cointreau and puree. Sandwich meringues together, placing the level one at the bottom and the peaked one on top. To decorate — sprinkle with toasted almonds, grated chocolate and then dust thickly with icing sugar. Freezes very well — thaw room temperature for 5 hours. Comes out as good as freshly made.

BLACKBERRY BOMBE

1 lb (450g) blackberries, fresh or frozen
4 oz (100g) granulated sugar
1 tablespoon (15ml) water
¼ pint (150ml) double cream
¼ pint (150ml) single cream
2½-3 oz (57g) broken meringue
SERVES 6

Cook berries with sugar in water until soft. Puree. Whip creams together until light, fluffy and holding shape. Fold in meringues. Add half a pint of blackberry puree (keeping rest for sauce), folding in carefully to keep a marbled effect. Turn mixture into a 2 pint (1.2 litre) pudding basin (preferably polythene with a lid). Cover and freeze. When required dip basin into hot water quickly. Turn out and pour remaining puree over top.

BLACKCURRANT MOUSSE

*12 oz (300g)
blackcurrants, fresh or
frozen
¼ pint (125ml) water
1 blackcurrant jelly
4 eggs
6 oz (150g) sugar
SERVES 6*

Stew blackcurrants in water until soft. Cut up jelly and stir into fruit until melted. Sieve mixture and leave to cool. Separate eggs. Beat yolks with sugar until light and fluffy. Stir into blackcurrant puree. Whisk egg whites stiffly and fold into mixture. Turn into a bowl and leave to set. Decorate with whipped cream if desired. Freezes well. Use any combination of fruit and appropriate jelly (even gooseberries and lemon jelly).

DREAMY CHOCOLATE TRIFLE

*4½ oz (125g) fresh brown
breadcrumbs
4 oz (100g) demerara
sugar
2 level tablespoons
(2x15ml) drinking
chocolate
2 level dessertspoons
(2x10ml) instant coffee
¼ pint (150ml) single
cream
¼ pint (150ml) double
cream
Chocolate flake for
decoration
SERVES 6*

Mix dry ingredients together. Whisk cream until smooth and thick. Line a serving bowl with half dry ingredients. Cover with layer of cream. Then add remainder of dry ingredients. Cover with remaining cream and decorate with chocolate flake etc. Refrigerate for 8-12 hours (overnight). Dry ingredients can be sprinkled with Tia Maria for that special occasion.

CHOCOLATE DATE NUT TORTE

6 oz (150g) sugar
2 oz (50g) finely grated
plain chocolate
4 oz (100g) chopped
walnuts
1 level teaspoon (5ml)
baking powder
¼ pint (150ml) whipped
cream
2 tablespoons (2x15ml)
plain flour
2 eggs
8 oz (225g) chopped dates
¼ teaspoon (1ml) cinnamon
SERVES 8

Oven Gas Mark 2, 300F, 150C. Sift flour and baking powder. Add 5 oz sugar. Beat the eggs until light. Add to dry ingredients (except cinnamon) and mix well. Fold in nuts, dates and chocolate. Put in greased 9 inch cake tin and sprinkle top of cake with remaining sugar and cinnamon. Cook for 30 minutes. Serve with whipped cream.

HAZELNUT BAVARIAN CREAM

½ pint (300ml) hot milk
2 eggs
2 oz (50g) caster sugar
2 oz (50g) icing sugar
½ oz (12g) gelatine
¼ pint (150ml) water
½ pint (300ml) double
cream
½ teaspoon vanilla essence
2 oz (50g) roasted chopped
hazelnuts
Sauce
¾ lb (300g) blackberries
2 oz (50g) sugar
¾ pint (450ml) water
SERVES 6

Simmer sauce items until fruit is soft. Sieve and cool. Melt gelatine in water. Separate eggs and place yolks and sugar in a double pan over hot water — not boiling. Add heated milk and stir continuously until thickens (at least 10 minutes). Gradually add gelatine and essence and cool. Beat egg whites until stiff but not dry. Add to mixture. Whip cream and mix in also. Add hazelnuts. Pour mixture into mould and set in fridge. Serve with blackcurrant sauce. Freezes well.

CHOCOLATE AND COFFEE MOUSSE

4 oz (100g) plain chocolate
4 eggs, separated
1 tablespoon (15ml) strong black coffee
1 tablespoon (15ml) rum or brandy
½ pint (150ml) cream
Chopped almonds
SERVES 4

Melt the chocolate in a bowl over a pan of simmering water. Beat the egg yolks with the coffee and rum, remove the chocolate from heat and stir in the egg yolk mixture. Whisk the whites and fold them into the chocolate mixture. Pour into individual glasses and chill. Decorate with whipped cream and chopped almonds.

CHOCOLATE PEPPERMINT GATEAU

2 bars peppermint Aero
3 tablespoons (3x15ml) milk
6 oz (175g) margarine
6 oz (175g) caster sugar
3 eggs, beaten
5 oz (150g) self raising flour
1 oz (25g) cocoa
Filling
¾ pint (450ml) double cream (whipped)
3 teaspoons (3x5ml) peppermint essence
1 box of After Eight Mints
1 Aero chocolate bar
SERVES 8-10

Cake: Dissolve two bars of Aero in milk over a basin of hot water. Cool. Cream margarine and sugar. Gradually beat in eggs. Sift flour and cocoa together and gradually fold into mixture alternately with chocolate and milk mixture. Divide between two 8 inch greased and lined tins and bake in moderate oven (Gas Mark 5, 375F, 190F) for 25 minutes. Allow to cool.

Filling: Combine whipped cream and peppermint essence. Cut the two cakes in half horizontally. Sandwich the four layers together using two thirds of the filling. Spread a little more of the filling round sides of cake.

Decoration : Dissolve Aero in basin over hot water. Spread over top of cake. Decorate sides by pressing After Eight Mints onto cream. Pipe whirls of remaining cream around top edge of cake and place a half After Eight Mint (triangle shape) between each whirl. This is rather expensive to make but it is delicious for that extra special occasion. The cost could be cut by using fewer mints for the decoration.

SPICED PEACHES

1 (420g) large tin sliced peaches
1 tablespoon (15ml) raisins
Good pinch cinnamon or mixed spice
Sherry (to taste)
Ice-cream
SERVES 8

Warm together peaches, raisins, spices and sherry in pan or microwave — not too hot. Serve into glasses. Top with ice-cream. Very easy, very quick. Desperate last minute dessert!

WHISKY CHOCOLATE MOUSSE

6 oz (175g) plain chocolate
4 eggs
1 teaspoon (5ml) vanilla essence
Grated rind of one orange
½ pint (284ml) double cream
3 tablespoons (45ml) whisky
Little grated chocolate
SERVES 6-8

Melt chocolate, allow to cool. Beat in egg yolks one at a time. Flavour with vanilla essence and orange rind. Whip cream, stir in whisky. Add to chocolate mixture. Beat egg whites and fold into chocolate mixture carefully. Serve in one large bowl or small dishes. Chill for 2 hours before serving. Decorate with grated chocolate.

CHOCOLATE SOUFFLÉ

3 eggs
½ lb (200g) plain chocolate
2 tablespoons (30ml) milk
3 oz (75g) caster sugar
½ oz (12g) gelatine
½ glass of water
½ pint (284ml) double cream
SERVES 6-8

Melt chocolate with milk, sugar and egg yolks in a pan. Stir until creamy. Mix gelatine with water and add to chocolate mixture. Whip cream and add to mixture. When cool fold in beaten egg whites. Turn into soufflè dish and chill in fridge. Decorate with chocolate shapes or grated dark chocolate.

TRUFFLE AND COFFEE ICE CREAM

4 oz (125g) plain chopped chocolate
2 tablespoons (30ml) single cream
2 tablespoons (30ml) rum
2 tablespoons (30ml) instant coffee
2 tablespoons (30ml) boiling water
2 egg whites
4 oz (125g) caster sugar
½ pint (284ml) double cream

Put the chocolate, single cream and rum in a heatproof bowl over a pan of simmering water until the chocolate has melted. Mix well and leave to cool. Meanwhile, make the ice cream. Dissolve the coffee in the boiling water and leave to cool. Whisk the egg whites until stiff, then gradually mix in the sugar. Whip the cream with the coffee until it forms soft peaks. Fold into the meringue mixture. When the truffle mixture begins to thicken, stir until smooth and soft. Fold into the ice cream mixture, very lightly to create a marbled effect. Turn into a rigid freezerproof container, cover, seal and freeze until firm. Transfer to the fridge 15 minutes before serving. This ice cream never goes hard and can be served straight from the freezer if necessary. Only serve small helpings as it is very rich. Goes well with oranges or raspberries or as a special treat — tinned lychees.

CHOCOLATE BOOZY WHIP

1 jam filled Swiss roll
2 tablespoons (30ml) instant coffee
4 tablespoons (60ml) boiling water
3 tablespoons (45ml) whisky or rum
8 oz (200g) plain chocolate
½ oz (13g) butter
4 eggs
SERVES 6

Cut Swiss roll into slices and place in bottom of a dish. Dissolve coffee in boiling water, add whisky or rum. Pour over Swiss roll and leave to soak. Melt chocolate, add butter and leave to cool. Separate eggs, beat yolks into chocolate. Whisk egg whites until stiff and fold into chocolate mixture. Pour over Swiss roll and leave to chill for at least two hours. Decorate with whipped cream before serving. Will freeze.

FROZEN LEMON CREAM

8 oz (225g) full fat soft
cheese
4 oz (100g) caster sugar
grated rind and juice of 2
lemons
2 egg yolks
½ pint (300ml) whipping
or double cream
SERVES 6-8

Soften cheese. Beat in sugar, lemon juice, rind
and egg yolks. Whip the cream until thick. Fold
into cheese mixture. Spoon into jelly mould.
Freeze until firm. Turn out onto plate and serve.

FRUIT FOOL

1 (135g) fruit jelly
½ pint (250ml) boiling
water
12 oz (300g) fruit, fresh
or frozen
2 oz (50g) sugar
(170g) small tin
evaporated milk
SERVES 6-8

Make jelly up to half a pint with boiling water.
Leave to cool, but not set. Stew fruit to a pulp
in very little water (if using frozen fruit, stew
straight from freezer, without any water added).
Add sugar and stir well. Leave to cool. Whisk
evaporated milk. Whisk into half-set jelly. Stir
into fruit mixture. Pour into a large bowl, or
individual dishes, and leave to set. Serve with
ice cream or fresh cream; or covered with
whipped cream and decorated as desired.

COLD LEMON SOUFFLÉ

3 large eggs
4½ oz (112g) caster sugar
1 large lemon
1 packet powdered gelatine
10 oz (300 fl oz)
whipping cream
2 oz (50g) flaked almonds
(optional)
SERVES 6

Separate eggs. Place yolks, sugar, grated lemon
rind and juice into a bowl, whisk until thick.
Put 2 tablespoons of cold water in a small bowl,
sprinkle on the gelatine, add 4 tablespoons
boiling water, leave to dissolve. Trickle dissolved
gelatine onto yolk mixture, beating all the time.
Whip cream until it forms soft peaks. Whisk
egg whites. When lemon mixture begins to set,
fold in cream and egg whites. Pour into a dish
and decorate. Chill in fridge. Will freeze.

SNOW QUEEN

½ pint (300ml) double cream
2 tablespoons (30ml) brandy
1 tablespoon (15ml) caster
sugar
4 oz (100g) meringue,
roughly broken
Raspberries to decorate
SERVES 8

Whisk cream until stiff. Stir in brandy and caster sugar. Fold in broken meringue. Taste and add more sugar if necessary. Pour the mixture into a lightly oiled 1 pint (600ml) pudding basin or bombe mould. Cover, seal and freeze for up to 2 months. To serve, unwrap, unmould place on serving dish and thaw for 15 minutes in fridge. Decorate.

CHOCOLATE CREAM PIE

Base
8 oz (225g) digestive,
wheatmeal, rich tea or
gingernut biscuits
5 oz (150g) butter
1-2 oz (25-50g) sugar
(optional)
Filling
½ pint (300ml) milk
1 oz (25g) caster sugar
1 oz (25g) plain flour
1½ level teaspoons (7.5ml)
cornflour
2 eggs
1 oz (25g) unsalted butter
3-3½ oz (75-100g) dark
plain chocolate, grated
2 teaspoons (2x5ml)
brandy or rum
Icing sugar
Topping
¼ pint (150ml) double cream
1 tablespoon (15ml) milk
Grated chocolate (optional)
SERVES 6-8

Crush the biscuits with a rolling pin in a plastic bag. Melt the butter in a saucepan and then add crumbs with sugar if used. Mix well and then spread into an 8 inch fluted flan case for 2 hours. Heat the milk. Blend sugar, flour, cornflour and beaten egg together in a bowl, then stir in milk. Return this mixture to the pan and cook over low heat, stirring continuously, until the mixture thickens and just comes to the boil. Remove the pan from the heat and stir in butter, cut into small pieces, the chocolate and brandy. Stir until smooth, then leave to cool slightly. Spoon the filling into the biscuit crust, and dust it with icing sugar to prevent a skin forming. Chill. Just before serving, whip the cream with the milk until thick enough to hold its shape. Spoon this in an even layer over the chocolate filling. Dust with coarsely grated chocolate.

EASY CHEESECAKE

4 oz (100g) crushed plain
biscuits
2 oz (50g) butter or
margarine, melted
Topping
1 tablespoon (15ml) icing
sugar
4 oz (100g) cream cheese
1 small carton double
cream or if preferred;
1 packet dream topping
mixed with less milk for a
thicker consistency
1 small tin fruit well
drained, if liked
Kiwi fruit and grated
chocolate to decorate
SERVES 4-6

Mix the crushed biscuits into melted butter or margarine. Press into 7 inch dish or foil lined tin and chill. Cream together the cheese and icing sugar. Beat in the whipped cream or the thick Dream Topping. Stir in fruit at this stage if desired. Pour over chilled base and chill for one hour. If made without fruit decorate with slices of kiwi fruit and grated chocolate.

LEMON GUNGE

4 oz (100g) digestive
biscuits
2 oz (50g) butter
1/4 level teaspoon ground
cinnamon
1/2 pint (300ml) whipping
cream
1 small tin condensed milk
2 medium lemons
Few chocolate buttons
SERVES 6

Crush biscuits. Melt butter in pan on low heat. Add biscuits and cinnamon. Press mixture into 8 inch flan dish. Grate lemon (reserve four thin slices for decoration) rind and squeeze juice from lemons. Beat cream until it thickens and add condensed milk. Add lemon juice and whip until mixture thickens again. Place mixture onto biscuit base. Sprinkle lemon rind on top. Decorate with lemon slices and chocolate buttons. Leave in fridge a few hours before serving.

BRANDY COFFEE PARADISE

6 oz (175g) butter
6 oz (175g) sugar
3 large eggs
2 tablespoons coffee essence
1 tablespoon brandy
12 sponge fingers
¼ pint (134ml) cream
SERVES 8

Line base and sides of 8 inch loose bottomed cake tin with greaseproof paper. Cream butter and sugar until fluffy, beat in eggs one at a time. Beat in coffee essence and brandy and more brandy if liked. Cut sponges in half lengthwise and arrange 8 pieces in base of tin. Pour in half of cream mixture, then rest of sponge. Press down and cover with a plate. Place weight on plate and leave in fridge at least 4 hours, overnight if possible. Turn out carefully and decorate with whipped cream.

BISCUIT TONTONI

½ pint (250ml) whipping or double cream
2 oz (50g) sieved icing sugar
1 egg white
2 tablespoons sherry
2 oz (50g) crushed ratafia biscuits
Few drops vanilla essence
SERVES 6

Beat cream until it forms swirls, then fold in icing sugar and vanilla essence. Whisk egg white until it forms peak. Fold into cream and finally stir in sherry and crushed biscuits. Spoon into either one container or individual dishes. Freeze for approximately 2 hours or until frozen. Remove from freezer only when required as it melts quickly. Can be decorated for serving with cream and a ratafia if wished.

ST CLEMENT'S TRIFLE

10 fl oz (280ml) double cream
1 oz (25g) icing sugar
6 trifle sponges
Rind and juice of 1 lemon and 2 oranges
Slices of lemon and orange
SERVES 6

Whip the cream, fold in the icing sugar, add the rind and juice from the fruit. Crumble the 6 sponges into the mixture and blend evenly through the cream. Place mixture into serving dish and chill for 2 hours. Decorate with whipped cream and lemon and orange slices.

BRAMBLE MOUSSE

1 lb (450g) blackberries
(stalks removed and
washed)
4 oz (125g) caster sugar
1 level tablespoon gelatine
2 tablespoons water
1 tablespoon lemon juice
¼ pint (125ml) double
cream
2 egg whites
SERVES 6-8

Put blackberries in pan (reserve a few whole ones for decoration) stir in sugar, simmer over low heat for 10-15 minutes or until blackberries are soft. Meanwhile sprinkle gelatine over water in small bowl and dissolve either by putting in microwave oven or placing bowl over hot water. Stir in lemon juice, (gelatine should not boil otherwise it does not set properly). Rub blackberries through a sieve into bowl. Stir in gelatine mixture, leave puree in cold place until beginning to set. Whip cream until thick, fold into blackberry puree. Whisk egg whites until stiff, fold into mousse until thoroughly combined. Pour into large serving bowl or individual glasses. Chill until set, decorate with blackberries and more cream if wished before serving.

CHOCOLATE CREAM

½ pint (250ml) single
cream
6 oz (175g) good dark
chocolate
2 egg yolks
Brandy
Chopped nuts and cream to
decorate
SERVES 6

Put pieces of chocolate in liquidiser or food processor to break up further. Add yolks and approximately 1 tablespoon of brandy (or to taste), turn on for a few seconds to mix in. Put cream in pan, bring almost to boil and pour immediately onto chocolate mixture. Turn on machine until chocolate has dissolved. Pour into a dish or individual glasses and leave to set in fridge for 2 hours. Decorate with cream and nuts.

CHOCOLATE NUT SUNDAE

Vanilla ice cream
Whipped cream
Chopped nuts
Chocolate sauce
2 oz (50g) plain chocolate
½ oz (13g) butter
1 tablespoon milk
1 teaspoon vanilla essence

To make sauce, melt chocolate and butter in basin over hot water (or in microwave oven). Stir in milk and vanilla essence to make a smooth creamy sauce. To assemble put scoops of ice cream into sundae glasses, pour chocolate sauce over. Pipe whipped cream on top, sprinkle with chopped nuts.

VARIATION PEAR BELL HÉLÈNE

Serve scoops vanilla ice cream with either tinned pear halves or whole poached fresh pears with chocolate sauce poured over top and decorated with whipped cream.

DANISH APPLE CHARLOTTE

8 oz (225g) breadcrumbs
3 oz (75g) soft brown sugar
2 oz (50g) butter or margarine
1½ lb (675g) cooking apples
Lemon juice and rind
Sugar to sweeten apples
¼ pint (125ml) cream
2 oz (50g) grated chocolate
SERVES 6

Melt butter or margarine in frying pan, add breadcrumbs and gently fry until crisp and browned. Stir in brown sugar. Stew apples with a little water, add lemon juice, rind and sugar to taste. Put alternate layers of apple and crumbs, finishing with crumbs. When cold spread top with whipped cream and sprinkle grated chocolate over. Serve cold.

GINGER GRUNDY

½ pint (300ml) fresh
double cream
2 oz (50g) butter
6 oz (175g) ginger
biscuits, crumbled
13 oz (375g) tin crushed
pineapple, drained
5 level tablespoons
marmalade
1½ level teaspoons ground
ginger
Whipped cream and stem
ginger to decorate
SERVES 6

Melt butter in saucepan, remove from heat and stir in 4 oz (125g) of the crushed biscuits. Mix well to coat in the butter. Rest a 8 inch flan ring on a flat plate or use a 8 inch flan dish. Press the buttered crumbs in a layer to coat the base, refrigerate. Whip the cream until thick and stir in the drained crushed pineapple, the marmalade and ginger. Spoon mixture over chilled ginger base. Scatter the top of the cream with the remaining ginger crumbs, chill well, remove ring and dust with icing sugar, decorate.

KIWI DELIGHT

1 jam Swiss roll
6 kiwi fruit peeled and
sliced
4 oz (125g) broken
macaroons
3 egg whites
4 oz (125g) caster sugar
5 fl oz (150ml) dry white
vermouth
2 tablespoons brandy
1 tablespoon lemon juice
10 fl oz (280ml) double
cream
SERVES 8

Slice the Swiss roll and place in glass serving dish, soak with the brandy. Place 5 of the kiwi fruit over the Swiss roll and place a few at the sides of the glass dish to show. Sprinkle the broken macaroons over the top. Whisk the egg whites with the sugar until firm and glossy, pour in the vermouth and lemon juice and gently fold through the meringue. Whip the fresh cream until softly stiff, leaving sufficient to pipe for decoration, combine the remainder of the cream with the meringue mixture, cover the base and chill for 2 hours. Finally decorate with whipped cream, slices of kiwi fruit, flaked almonds and maraschino cherries.

LEMON GRIESTORTE

3 eggs
4 oz (125g) caster sugar
Rind and juice of half a
lemon
2 oz (50g) semolina
½ oz (13g) ground
almonds
½ pint (250ml) cream
½ jar lemon curd
(preferably home-made)
Icing sugar and grated
chocolate
SERVES 8

Grease and line 8 inch cake tin. Dust sides with sugar, then flour. Separate eggs, work yolks and sugar with wooden spoon or in mixer until light in colour and thick. Add lemon juice, beat again. Stir in lemon rind, semolina and ground almonds. Whisk egg whites until stiff, fold into lemon mixture. Pour into cake tin and bake for 40-45 minutes in oven at Gas Mark 4, 350F, 180C. Do not open oven door until cake has been baking for at least 25-30 minutes. When cake is cold, split and fill with whipped cream and lemon curd. Dust with icing sugar and finely grated chocolate.

Variation: Fill with sliced fresh or tinned pears and cream.

LEMON PARADISE

14 oz (400g) tin
condensed milk
3 lemons, grated rind and
juice
3 large eggs, separated
1 packet trifle sponges or 1
packet Boudoir biscuits
SERVES 8

Lightly grease a 2 lb loaf tin and line with cling film. Stir lemon rind, juice and egg yolks into the condensed milk. Whisk egg whites until stiff, then fork into lemon mixture which should be beginning to thicken. Cut sponges in half to make them thinner. Place a quarter of them in tin and spoon over half the lemon mixture. Continue layering ending with sponge. Cover with cling film and refrigerate for at least two days, (three to four days even better). Carefully remove from tin and decorate with cream and sliced lemon (or as desired). A delicious sweet for a dinner party or any occasion as it can be made a few days in advance.

MERINGUE

2 egg whites
4 oz (125g) caster sugar

Whisk egg whites until stiff, gradually add the sugar, continue beating until the mixture is smooth and will stand in a peak when the beater is removed from the mixture. Mixture is now ready for use. To prepare baking sheets, grease tin then cover with non stick baking paper, pipe on meringues. Cook the meringue in a very slow heat, 70C, 140F, ¼ Gas for about 5 hours. Cool and use, or store in an air tight container.

MERINGUE BASKETS

Fruit
Fresh cream whipped

The basic quantity should be sufficient for 6 individual baskets. Prepare baking sheet, draw 2½ inch circles approximately 2 inch apart onto the underside of the paper for a guide. Using a quarter or half-inch star tube, starting from the centre pipe the circle. Pipe one more circle directly on top of the outer circle. Using the tube to produce a star, place a star all the way round the top. Bake as before. Using fruit of your own choice and whipped cream, spoon a little cream into basket, top with fruit and serve.

PEACH GATEAU

4 eggs
4 oz (125g) self raising flour
4 oz (125g) caster sugar
2 oz (50g) butter
6 oz (175g) peach preserve
2x15½ oz (438g) peach halves
arrowroot
Sponge fingers
Green ribbon
½ pint (250ml) double cream
SERVES 7

To prepare base, whisk eggs and sugar until double in bulk and the whisk leaves a trail in the mixture. Gently fold in the flour, then gently fold in the cooled melted butter. Pour the mixture into 2 prepared 7 inch sandwich tins, bake at Gas Mark 4, 350F, 180C. for 30 minutes approximately. To prepare the decoration, whip the cream and place half in a piping bag with small star tube. Drain peach halves keeping 6 whole, chop remainder and combine with cream. Beat the peach preserve for easier spreading. Using the fruit juice blend a little arrowroot with the juice, bring remaining juice to boil, add the arrowroot and boil, stirring continuously until clear, allow to cool slightly. To assemble the gateau, split the 2 cakes, spread with peach preserve between the first and third layers. Middle layer place the cream and chopped peaches. Pipe a little cream onto sponge fingers and arrange round the outside of the cake. To help hold in position tie the ribbon round the centre. Place the peach halves on top of the cake in a ring of 5 with 1 peach half in the centre, coat completely with fruit glaze. When set, pipe rosettes of cream in all exposed cake areas.

RASPBERRY SYLLABUB

8 oz (225g) raspberries
2 tablespoons cointreau or grand marnier
1 glass sweet white wine
2 oz (50g) caster sugar
½ pint (250ml) double cream
SERVES 4

Bruise half raspberries with wooden spoon, sprinkle with half sugar and Cointreau. Divide this mixture into individual wine glasses. Whisk the cream with remaining sugar until stiff, gradually add wine, whisking all the time. Fold in remaining raspberries. Spoon this mixture on top of raspberries in the glasses. Chill and serve.

Chapter Eleven

Tea Breads and Yeast Cookery

WORKING WITH YEAST

Fresh yeast is pale fawn in colour and pliable in texture, and on ageing, it will become more grey and crumbly. It should not be used if it smells fusty or has become brown in colour. Store in a cool place in a polythene bag or screw top jar, the fresher the yeast, the more active it is. Yeast may also be stored in small quantities in a deep freeze.

Sponging — Cream the yeast with a little sugar in a bowl, add the lukewarm liquid and a little of the flour, cover and leave in a warm place until a good froth has formed — this allows the yeast to become active in ideal conditions and it will continue to work more vigorously.

Dried yeast — "Easy Blend" dried yeast is very convenient, and is simply mixed into the flour (no sponging necessary). Check manufacturer's instructions regarding quantities.

Temperature — This is an important factor in yeast mixtures. Plain bread, if intended to be kept, will give best results (other things being equal) at a temperature of 70-75F. A richer mixture will benefit by a warmer temperature 80-90F. If a dough is made in sufficient bulk and the room temperature is from 65-70F, it will not be chilled as long as it is protected from draughts. A large polythene bag is excellent for this. The cooler the mixture the longer time taken for proving, in fact it can be made up cold and left in a polythene bag overnight at room temperature and completed next morning.

SHOWING BREAD

White

Schedule should state size of loaf and whether a "tin" shape is required. If so the type of tin usually made for bread making gives the best shape. Loaf should be well risen and evenly baked. Warm golden brown in colour. Base should be free from shaping cracks, base and corners should be clean. Internal texture should be light, fine and even — no holes or streaks. Should be soft and springy to touch and should not crumble if stroked gently. Well developed flavour, sufficient salt. No stale or sour flavour.

Wholemeal

Should be 100% wholemeal flour. The texture will be closer than white bread and it would be less well risen.

Wheatmeal or brown

Is made from flours of 85-90% extraction and has a lighter texture and better rise than wholemeal.

Bread rolls

Should be light, well risen, even in size, shape and texture. No shaping cracks on base, any glazing should be even, not patchy.

TROUBLESHOOTING

A "flying top" when top crust breaks away from loaf	Under proving. Dough surface dried out during proving. Oven too hot.
Crust surface cracks after removal from oven	Over proving. Oven too hot. Cooling in draught after baking.
Dough collapses when put into oven	Over proving.
Heavy close texture	Flour too soft. Too much salt.
Poor volume	Insufficient kneading or proving. Yeast killed by rising in too hot a place.
Coarse open texture	Too much liquid/salt. Over proving.
Sour yeasty flavour and smell of alcohol.	Over proving. Too much yeast. Stale yeast.

WHITE BREAD

3 ½ lb (1.75kg) flour
6 level teaspoons salt
1 oz (25g) yeast
1 ½ pints (900ml) lukewarm water

Sieve flour into warm bowl and set aside in warm place. Divide water into two, dissolve salt in one part and whisk yeast into other. Mix the two and add to flour, mixing to a dough with hands. Turn on to a floured board and knead well for 5 minutes. Return to bowl to prove. Turn dough on to floured board, knead lightly, then divide into four portions. Mould into shape, place in greased tins and prove. Bake at Gas Mark 7, 425F, 220C for about 40 minutes.

QUICK BROWN BREAD

12 oz (350g) wholemeal flour
4 oz (125g) strong plain flour
2 level teaspoons salt
1 sachet of fast action dried yeast
½ pint (300ml) lukewarm water
½ oz lard (optional)
1 teaspoon malt extract (optional, dissolved in the water)

Put both flours, salt and lard in food processor, blend well, add the yeast, blend, use sufficient lukewarm water to give a soft spongy dough. Process for approx. 1 minute until well kneaded. Turn onto a floured table, shape into a loaf, cob or rolls, place on greased tins or tray, cover with polythene bag and put in warm place to prove until twice original size. Bake loaf or cob at Gas Mark 7, 425F, 220C, turn down after 15 minutes, bake until sounds hollow when tapped (approx. further 15-20 minutes). Rolls, bake at Gas Mark 7, 425F, 220C for about 15 minutes.

YEAST DOUGH BISCUITS

8 oz (225g) white bread dough
8 oz (225g) porridge oats
3 oz (75g) lard
3 oz (75g) caster sugar
1 level teaspoon baking powder
1 level teaspoon salt
½ teaspoon bicarbonate of soda

When dough for bread is fully risen (i.e. when ready to put into tins after first proving) weigh out ½ lb (225g) and put into a bowl. Add lard, sugar, oats, baking powder, salt and bicarbonate of soda. Knead until all ingredients have worked together. Roll out to ¼ inch thickness and cut out using a fairly large plain cutter. Put on greased tin and bake at Gas Mark 6, 400F, 200C, until pale brown. This savoury biscuit can be served with butter, cheese or savoury spread.

YORKSHIRE TEACAKES

2 lb (1kg) flour
2 teaspoons salt
2 oz (50g) lard
2 oz (50g) currants
2 oz (50g) sugar
1 oz (25g) yeast
1 pint (600ml) tepid milk
and water

Sieve flour and salt in warm bowl. Cream yeast with sugar. Pour the warm milk on the yeast. Rub lard into flour, add currants. Pour yeast and milk slowly into flour and mix to a light dough. Knead well and set to rise in a warm place. When well risen form into small cakes and place on greased baking sheet. Put into a warm place to rise again for 30 minutes. Bake in a quick oven for 10 minutes. Gas Mark 7, 425F, 220C. Rub over with a lard paper.

OLD FASHIONED YULE BREAD

1½ lb (750g) plain flour
1 teaspoon salt
2 teaspoons baking powder
4 oz (125g) lard
4 oz (125g) butter
8 oz (225g) brown moist
sugar
1 lb (450g) currants
4 oz (125g) peel
2 oz (50g) yeast
1 lb (450g) sultanas or
raisins

Rub fat into flour, salt and baking powder, add sugar and fruit. Cream yeast with a little sugar, add warm milk with the beaten egg. Add to dry ingredients. Mix well together and divide into bread tins. Put in a warm place for 20-30 minutes. Bake at Gas Mark 4, 350F, 180C for 15 minutes, reduce to Gas Mark 2, 300F, 150C for 45 minutes.

HOT CROSS BUNS

1 lb (450g) plain flour
1 teaspoon salt
1 teaspoon allspice
1 teaspoon nutmeg
3 oz (75g) sugar
2 oz (50g) butter
4 oz (125g) currants
2 oz (50g) peel
1 oz (25g) yeast
1 beaten egg
¼ pint (150ml) tepid milk

Rub butter into dry ingredients, add fruit. Cream yeast in 1 teaspoon sugar and pour into a well made in centre. Add milk and beaten egg and mix well. Either cut into pieces and make buns or roll 1 inch thick and cut with cutter. Make a cross on each. Bake on greased tray at Gas Mark 7, 425F, 220C for 15 minutes. Glaze when taken from oven with 2 tablespoons sugar boiled in 2 tablespoons milk.

HARVO TEA BREAD

12 oz (350g) self raising flour
6 oz (175g) sugar
6½ fl oz (188ml) water
½ teaspoon salt
5 oz (150g) margarine
5 oz (150g) sultanas
1½ level teaspoons bicarbonate of soda

Simmer together margarine, sugar, sultanas and water for a few minutes. Mix with dry ingredients and put into a greased 2 lb loaf tin. Bake at Gas Mark 1, 275F or 140C for 1 hour 30 minutes.

SKEEBY MALT LOAF

12 fl oz (350ml) hot water
13 oz (375g) sultanas
2 oz (50g) butter
13 oz (375g) self raising flour
2 oz (50g) chopped walnuts
9 oz (250g) sugar
2 beaten eggs
½ teaspoon bicarbonate soda

Simmer together water, butter and sultanas for 4 minutes, cool. Mix together walnuts, flour, bicarbonate of soda and sugar. Mix flour and fruit mixture together and add beaten eggs. Place in greased and lined 2x1 lb (500g) loaf tins. Bake in a moderate oven Gas Mark 5, 375F, 190C for 1 hour.

BRAN LOAF

2 breakfast cups All Bran
2 breakfast cups brown sugar
2 breakfast cups mixed fruit
2 breakfast cups milk
2 breakfast cups self raising
flour
1 egg

Mix first four ingredients in a large bowl, leave to stand overnight, then mix in self raising flour and egg. Mix well and put into a 2 lb loaf tin. Bake for 1 hour 30 minutes at Gas Mark 4, 350F, 180C.

ORANGE RAISIN LOAF

12 oz (350g) self raising
flour
1 level teaspoon bicarbonate
of soda
2 oz (50g) lard
Rind and juice of 1 orange,
2 eggs and milk mixed
together to make 300ml of
liquid
2 oz (50g) margarine
8 oz (225g) caster sugar
8 oz (225g) raisins

Rub the fats into dry ingredients. Add the raisins and the liquid and mix together. Drop into 2x1 lb greased loaf tins and bake in a moderate oven Gas Mark 3, 325F, 160-170C for approximately 1 hour. Serve sliced and buttered.

HARVEST FRUIT LOAF

4 oz (125g) margarine
4 oz (125g) sugar
8 oz (225g) self raising
flour
12 oz (350g) mixed dried
fruit
1 level teaspoonful mixed
spice
2 eggs beaten with ¼ pint
(125ml) milk

Place all ingredients together into bowl, beat for 2 to 3 minutes. Divide into 2 well greased 1 lb loaf tins, and bake for approximately 1 hour 30 minutes at Gas Mark 3, 325F, 160C. Served sliced and buttered.

DATE AND WALNUT CAKE

7 fl oz (210ml) boiling
water
6 oz (175g) dates, chopped
3/4 level teaspoon
bicarbonate of soda
6 oz (175g) dark brown
sugar
2 oz (50g) margarine or
butter
1 egg, beaten
8 oz (225g) self raising
flour
2 oz (50g) walnuts,
chopped

Heat the oven to Gas Mark 4, 350F, 180C.
Grease and line an 8 inch (20cm) square cake
tin with greased greaseproof paper. Measure the
water, dates and bicarbonate of soda into a bowl
and leave to stand for about 5 minutes. Put the
sugar and margarine into a bowl and cream
together, then beat in the egg and the date
mixture. Fold in the flour together with the
walnuts and mix lightly until thoroughly
blended. Turn the mixture into the tin and level
out evenly. Bake in the oven for about an hour
until risen and slightly shrinking away from the
sides of the tin. A skewer should come out clean
when pushed into the centre of the cake.

BANANA CHERRY LOAF

8 oz (225g) self raising
flour
4 oz (100g) margarine or
butter
6 oz (175g) caster sugar
4 oz (100g) glace cherries,
quartered
2 large bananas, mashed
2 eggs, beaten
MAKES 2 LOAVES

Heat the oven to Gas Mark 4, 350F, 180C.
Grease and line two 1 lb (450g) loaf tins with
greased greaseproof paper. Measure all the
ingredients into a bowl and mix well until
thoroughly blended. Divide the mixture
between the two tins and level out evenly. Bake
in the oven for about 1 hour until well risen. A
skewer should come out clean when pushed into
the centre of the loaves. Leave to cool in the
tins for 2-3 minutes, then turn out, peel off
paper and finish the cooling on a wire rack.

MINCEMEAT FRUIT LOAVES

2 eggs
5 oz (150g) caster sugar
5 oz (150g) soft
margarine
8 oz (225g) self raising
flour
12 oz (350g) mincemeat
8 oz (225g) currants
A few flakes almonds
MAKES 2 LOAVES

Heat the oven to Gas Mark 3, 325F, 160C. Grease and line two 1 lb (450g) loaf tins with greased greaseproof paper. Crack the eggs into a large roomy bowl, then add all the other ingredients. Mix well until blended. Divide the mixture between the two tins and level out evenly. Sprinkle with flaked almonds. Bake in the oven for about 1 hour 15 minutes until risen, pale golden brown and shrinking away from the sides of the tin. A fine skewer pushed into the centre of the loaves should come out clean. Turn out of the tins and cool on a wire rack.

APRICOT FRUIT LOAF

2 large eggs
4 oz (100g) self raising flour
3 oz (75g) margarine or
butter
3 oz (75g) light brown sugar
2 oz (50g) glace cherries,
quartered
3 oz (75g) apricot pieces
3 oz (75g) sultanas

Heat the oven to Gas Mark 3, 325F, 160C. Grease and line a 1 lb (450g) loaf tin with greased greaseproof paper. Break the eggs into a large bowl, add all the other ingredients, and beat well until smooth. Turn into the prepared tin and level the top. Bake in the oven for about an hour until golden brown and shrinking away from the sides of the tin. A fine skewer pushed into the centre of the cake should come out clean.

MRS WATSON'S FRUIT LOAF

10 oz (275g) plain flour
8 oz (225g) brown sugar
8 oz (225g) margarine
2 eggs
8 oz (225g) currants
8 oz (225g) sultanas
4 oz (125g) mixed peel
Small tin evaporated milk
Small teaspoon baking
powder

Rub margarine into flour. Add all other ingredients. Bake in two greased 1 lb loaf tins at Gas Mark 3, 325F, 160C for approximately 1 hour.

DAMP GINGERBREAD

12 oz (350g) syrup
4½ oz (135g) margarine
9 oz (250g) flour
½ teaspoon salt
1¾ teaspoons bicarbonate
of soda
1 heaped teaspoon ground
ginger
1 egg
½ pint (300ml) milk

Melt syrup and margarine. Pour on to dry ingredients and beat well. Add egg and milk gradually. Pour into well greased dripping tin, approximately 8x12 inch lined with paper and bake in a moderate oven for about fifty minutes. Gas Mark 3, 325F, 160C.

FRUIT SCONES

8 oz (225g) flour
2 oz (50g) lard
2 oz (50g) sugar
1 teaspoons cream of tartar
½ teaspoon bicarbonate soda
2 oz (50g) currants or
sultanas
1 egg
Milk

Rub fat into flour, add sugar and cream of tartar, bicarbonate of soda and fruit. Beat eggs and add a little milk. Stir in with a knife to make a soft dough. Add more milk if necessary. Roll out on floured board to half-inch thickness and cut into rounds. Place on a greased baking sheet and bake for approximately 10 minutes on shelf in a hot oven. Gas Mark 7, 425F, 220C.

YORKSHIRE SCONES

12 oz (350g) plain flour
2 tablespoons sugar
2 small teaspoons
bicarbonate of soda
2 heaped teaspoons cream
of tartar
Pinch salt
4 oz (125g) butter or
margarine
A little milk

Sieve flour, cream of tartar, bicarbonate of soda and salt together. Rub fat into flour, then stir in the sugar. Mix to a soft dough with a little milk. Roll out lightly on floured board. Cut into rounds. Place on greased baking tray and bake in a hot oven Gas Mark 8, 450F, 230C for 10-15 minutes. Makes 20-24 scones.

FAT RASCALS

8 oz (225g) self raising
flour
2 oz (50g) butter
2 oz (50g) lard
Milk to mix.
½ teaspoon salt
3 oz (75g) currants
3 oz (75g) sugar

Rub fat into flour, add salt. Add sugar and currants, mix well. Add sufficient milk to mix to the consistency of shortcrust pastry. Roll out, cut into rounds and bake in a hot oven at Gas Mark 6, 400F, 200C for about 15 minutes.

WHOLEMEAL NUT AND DATE SCONES

12 oz (350g) wholemeal
flour
2 oz (50g) sugar
3 teaspoons baking powder
3 oz (75g) margarine
1 teaspoon salt
1 beaten egg
½ pint (300ml) milk
2 oz (50g) chopped dates
2 oz (50g) chopped
walnuts

Mix flour, sugar, baking powder and salt. Rub in margarine. Add egg and milk then dates and nuts. Roll out and cut into scones. Bake in a moderate oven for 10-15 minutes at Gas Mark 6, 400F, 200C.

DROP SCONES OR SCOTCH PANCAKES

5 oz (150g) plain flour
2½ oz (75g) sugar
1 teaspoon (5ml)
bicarbonate of soda
1 teaspoon (5ml) cream of
tartar
1 egg
Milk to mix

Sieve flour, bicarbonate of soda and cream of tartar, add sugar. Beat in egg, then milk and beat with a wooden spoon until the batter is smooth and creamy. Drop dessertspoons of mixture onto a well greased griddle and cook for 1-2 minutes each side.

Chapter Twelve

Pastries and Tray Bakes

SHORT PASTRY

8 oz (225g) plain flour
2 oz (50g) lard
2 oz (50g) margarine or butter
⅛ pint (75ml) cold water
1 level teaspoon salt

Sieve the flour and salt into bowl and rub in the fat using finger tips. When this is like fine breadcrumbs add sufficient cold water to bind the ingredients with a knife into a stiff paste. Too much water will give a hard pastry. Generally can be used for many sweet and savoury dishes. Bake in the middle of a hot oven Gas Mark 8, 450F, 230C. This pastry can be made in a food processor. Put all dry ingredients and fats in bowl, blend for 10 seconds. Add water, blend to combine.

PUFF PASTRY

6 oz (175g) plain flour
Pinch of salt
6 oz (175g) butter
Approx. ¼ pint (150ml) ice cold water

Sieve the flour and salt together in a bowl. Rub in a walnut of butter. Add sufficient water to mix to a firm dough. Roll out to an oblong about half-inch (1cm) thick. The butter should be firm; not soft, not hard. Put the butter, shaped into an oblong pat, on to the lower half of the dough. Fold the top half down. Press the edges together. Leave to cool for 15-20 minutes. With the sealed ends towards you, roll lightly but firmly away from you into the original oblong. Do not 'push'. Fold the pastry into three; bottom third upwards and top third downwards. Turn the open end towards you. Roll out again to an oblong. Repeat folding and rolling process twice more. Fold in three again and leave to rest and relax before using. This pastry freezes well and can also be kept in the refrigerator wrapped in a dampish cloth for two to three days. Puff pastry is cooked at Gas Mark 7-8, 425-450F, 220-230C.

CHEESE PASTRY

8 oz (225g) flour
4-6 oz (125-175g) fat
(lard and margarine)
4-8 oz (125-225g) cheese
(according to taste)
1 egg yolk and water to
make ¼ pint (150ml)
Pinch cayenne pepper
⅛ teaspoon mustard

Sieve all dry ingredients. Rub in fat. Add grated cheese (hard cheese is the best). Make into a stiff dough with the egg and water. Cool and allow to relax after shaping. Bake in a moderate oven Gas Mark 4, 325-350F, 160C. Use for canapés, savoury flans, straws etc.

CHOUX PASTRY

5 oz (150g) plain flour
4 oz (125g) butter
3 large eggs
½ level teaspoon salt
½ pint (300ml) water

Heat the water and butter together. Sieve the flour and salt. Add all at once to the hot water and butter with the pan off the source of heat. Beat until the mixture forms a ball and leaves the sides of the pan. Cool. Add the beaten eggs gradually until a piping consistency is obtained. Pipe onto a greased baking sheet. Use ¼ inch pipe for buffet sized eclairs and puffs. Bake at Gas Mark 8, 450F, 230C until the pastry is dried through and is crisp and golden brown. Split open and cool on wire trays.

ALMOND SLICES

4 oz (125g) sugar
½ dessertspoon ground rice
Blanched almonds and
cherries for the top
2 oz (50g) ground
almonds
1 egg white (NOT beaten)
Raspberry jam

Line a Battenburg tin with short pastry and spread with raspberry jam. Mix all ingredients together and sprinkle almonds and cherries (chopped, on the top). Bake for 45 minutes, Gas Mark 4, 350F, 180C. (Double up for Swiss roll tin).

APPLE CHEESE CAKES

Shortcrust pastry
1 lb (450g) apples
3 oz (75g) butter
Rind and juice of 1 lemon
3 oz (75g) sugar
2 eggs

Peel and slice apples, stew in a very little water, add sugar and butter, grated rind and juice — cool slightly — then add the beaten eggs. Line 2 sandwich tins with pastry and fill with the mixture. Bake in a moderate oven. Gas Mark 4, 350F, 180C, for approximately 30 minutes. Reduce heat if necessary. Can be cooked as small tarts.

CHERRY SLICES

6 oz (175g) shortcrust pastry
4 oz (125g) ground almonds
4 oz (125g) glace cherries, chopped
4 oz (125g) butter
2 oz (50g) self raising flour
4 oz (125g) currants
4 oz (125g) sugar
2 eggs, beaten

Roll out pastry and line Swiss roll tin. Cream butter and sugar, add dry ingredients and stir in beaten eggs. Spread over pastry and bake at Gas Mark 4, 350F, 180C for 30-40 minutes, until golden brown and firm to touch. Leave to cool and cut into slices.

CURD TARTS

8 oz (225g) curds
3 tablespoons sugar
1 egg
Walnut of butter
2 oz (50g) currants
A little candied peel and lemon rind (optional)
A little nutmeg or rum
1 teaspoon baking powder

Mash up the curds and add dried fruit and flavouring. Add the well whisked egg, lastly the melted butter. Line saucers with shortcrust pastry and put the filling in. Bake in hot oven, Gas Mark 6, 400F, 200C, until golden brown. One tablespoon of golden syrup added in place of some sugar makes a shiny finish.

FRUIT CHEESE CAKES

Shortcrust pastry
4 oz (125g) cooking apples
2 oz (50g) currants
4 oz (125g) sugar
4 oz (125g) melted butter
Grated rind and juice of 1 lemon
2 well beaten eggs

Peel, core and finely chop apples, add other ingredients and bake in pastry case or as small tarts at Gas Mark 6, 400F, 200C for 35-40 minutes. Leave until pastry is cooled.

ORANGE SQUARES

8 oz (225g) shortcrust pastry
1 oz (25g) sugar
1 orange
A little granulated sugar
1 oz (25g) margarine
6 oz (175g) currants

Roll out half the pastry to line a Swiss roll tin. Melt the margarine and mix with the sugar and currants. Finely grate the orange rind. Remove the pith and chop the orange flesh. Mix chopped orange and rind with the currant mixture and spread over pastry. Damp edges, roll out rest of pastry to fit the tin. Cover and seal edges well. Mark in a criss-cross pattern. Brush with water and sprinkle with granulated sugar. Bake for 25-30 minutes on second shelf, Gas Mark 5, 370F, 190C.

RICE CHEESECAKES

4 oz (125g) butter
8 oz (225g) sugar
2 eggs
4 oz (125g) ground rice
1 oz (25g) currants
1 lemon grated rind and juice
8 oz (225g) shortcrust pastry

Cream the butter and sugar, beat in the eggs. Fold in the ground rice and currants and the lemon juice and rind. Line tartlet tins with shortcrust pastry and put a teaspoon of mixture on each circle of pastry. Bake in a quick oven Gas Mark 7, 425F, 220C for 20 minutes.

LEMON TART

1 uncooked shortcrust
pastry case
2 eggs
1 cup sugar
2 oz (50g) melted
margarine
1 dessertspoon ground rice
Juice and rind of 1 lemon

Beat eggs and add other ingredients. Pour into pastry case and bake at Gas Mark 5, 375F, 190C for approximately 30 minutes. Reduce heat if necessary.

CHERRY ALMOND SLICES

4 oz (100g) shortcrust
pastry
Red jam
3 oz (75g) ground
almonds
4 oz (100g) caster sugar
2 oz (50g) chopped glace
cherries
2 egg whites

Line a Swiss roll tin with the pastry and spread thinly with the jam. Mix together the ground almonds, sugar, cherries and egg whites, and spread over the pastry with wetted fingers. Bake at Gas Mark 5, 375F, 190C for 30-35 minutes. Mark into slices when cool, and cut when cold. If wished, sprinkle with flaked or chopped almonds when taken out of the oven.

ALMOND AND CHERRY BARS

8 oz (225g) shortcrust
pastry
4 oz (100g) margarine
4 oz (100g) caster sugar
2 oz (50g) ground
almonds
1 tablespoon (15ml)
ground rice
1 beaten egg
4 oz (100g) sultanas
2 oz (50g) chopped walnuts
2 oz (50g) cherries

Line a Swiss roll tin with pastry, partly cook for 5-10 minutes at Gas Mark 2, 300F, 150C. Cream margarine and sugar, add almonds, ground rice and eggs and beat well, add fruit and nuts and spread mixture over the pastry. Cook for a further 30-35 minutes at Gas Mark 4, 350F, 180C. Cool and sprinkle with sugar and cut into bars.

ALMOND SQUARES

Pastry
6 oz (170g) plain flour
1 tablespoon (15ml) icing sugar
3 oz (75g) lard and margarine mixed
½ teaspoon (2.5ml) salt
1½ tablespoons (25ml) water
Fillings
2 egg whites
4 oz (100g) ground almonds
2 oz (50g) ground rice
6 oz (170g) caster sugar
4 tablespoons (60ml) raspberry jam
2 oz (50g) flaked almonds
Swiss roll tin 12x8 inch (30x20cm)

Sift flour, salt and icing sugar together, rub in fat, mix with water. Roll out, line tin with pastry and stand in a cool place. Put egg whites into bowl and break up with fork, add ground almonds, ground rice and sugar, mix to a smooth paste with water. Spread pastry in tin with jam and cover with almond mixture. Sprinkle top with flaked almonds. Bake on centre shelf Gas Mark 5, 375F, 190C for 30-35 minutes. Makes 24.

ALMOND SLICE VARIATION

4 oz (100g) caster sugar
4 oz (100g) icing sugar
4 oz (100g) ground almonds
Few flaked almonds
2 oz (50g) semolina
1 egg and 1 egg white
Almond essence
6 oz (175g) plain flour
3 oz (75g) margarine
1 egg yolk
1 dessertspoon (10ml) caster sugar

Rub fat into flour and sugar, add egg yolk. Roll out and line flat tin with pastry. Mix icing sugar, ground almonds and semolina, add egg yolk, almond essence and a little water. Beat egg whites, add caster sugar, continue beating. Fold in other ingredients. Spread on pastry. Sprinkle with flaked almonds. Bake at Gas Mark 2, 300F, 150C for 30 minutes. Cut into fingers when cold.

AUSTRALIAN SHORTBREAD

6 oz (175g) butter
2 oz (50g) sugar
2 tablespoons (30ml)
syrup
8 oz (225g) quaker oats

Warm butter, sugar and syrup in pan. Mix with oats and bake in a shallow tin Gas Mark 4, 350F, 180C for about 30 minutes until golden brown. Cut before really cold.

APPLE TRAY BAKE

4 oz (100g) margarine
4 oz (100g) caster sugar
1 large egg beaten
8 oz (225g) self raising
flour
Pinch of salt
8 oz (225g) cooking apples
4 tablespoons (60ml) milk

Brush Swiss roll tin 10x8 inch (25x20cm) with melted fat. Cream margarine well before adding sugar, beat until fluffy, add beaten egg and beat again. Sieve flour and salt together. Peel, core and roughly chop apple, add to mixture along with milk. Turn into tin and level with a palette knife. Cook on centre shelf of oven Gas Mark 4, 350F, 180C for 25-30 minutes or until cake is golden brown and springy to the touch. Remove from oven and dredge with caster sugar. Cool then cut into 18 pieces.

APPLE SLICE SQUARES

4 oz (100g) self raising
flour
4 oz (100g) margarine
4 oz (100g) caster sugar
1 oz (25g) demerara sugar
2 large eggs beaten
Few drops almond essence
2 eating apples

Lightly grease a 13x9 inch (33x23cm) Swiss roll tin with melted fat. Line the base with a piece of greaseproof paper brushed with melted fat. Beat margarine until soft, add sugar and cream well together. Gradually add the beaten egg, stirring well after each addition. Add almond essence. Sift the flour and using a metal spoon fold into the creamed mixture. Spread over the base of the tin as evenly as possible. Peel, quarter and core the apples, and cut them into 36 slices. Arrange the slices in groups of 3 on the sponge mixture, sprinkle with demerara sugar and bake centre shelf Gas Mark 4, 350F, 180C. for 40 minutes.

BOSTON BROWNIES

4 oz (100g) margarine
3 oz (75g) plain cooking chocolate
6 oz (175g) self raising flour
6 oz (175g) soft brown sugar
2 large eggs beaten
3 oz (75g) salted peanuts

Lightly grease a 12x18 inch (30x45cm) Swiss roll tin and line with greaseproof paper also greased. Melt margarine, chocolate and sugar in a saucepan over a low heat. Remove pan from heat and stir mixture until well blended. Gradually add beaten eggs, stirring well between each addition. Mix peanuts with the flour and stir into the mixture, which should be quite wet in consistency. Pour mixture in prepared tin, bake Gas Mark 5, 375F, 190C for 20-25 minutes until mixture is firm and well risen. Cool slightly in the tin and cut into squares and put on wire tray.

BROKEN BISCUIT FINGERS

8 oz (225g) broken biscuits
2 oz (50g) sugar
1 egg
2 oz (50g) margarine
1 oz (25g) cocoa
½ oz (15g) nuts or cherries

Melt margarine, sugar and cocoa. Stir well, add beaten egg, cook 2 minutes in pan, add biscuits and nuts or cherries. This recipe does not need cooking. Press mixture into a tin and cut while warm.

COCONUT TRUFFLE BARS

4 oz (100g) margarine
4 oz (100g) icing sugar
2 oz (50g) cocoa
2 tablespoons (30ml) rum
6 oz (175g) coconut
10 oz (275g) mixed fruit (peel, nuts, ginger, cherries etc.)

Cream margarine and icing sugar, add cocoa, rum, coconut and mixed fruit. Press into a tin. Refrigerate until needed.

CHOCOLATE FINGERS

4 oz (100g) margarine
2 oz (50g) sugar
4 oz (100g) self raising flour
3 oz (75g) coconut
2 tablespoons (10ml) cocoa
5 oz (125g) cooking chocolate

Cream in fat and sugar, work in flour, coconut and cocoa. Spread in a Swiss roll tin 12x8 inch (30x20cm) about ¼ inch (5mm) thick. Bake at Gas Mark 4, 350F, 180C for 30 minutes. Before cold spread with melted cooking chocolate.

CHOCOLATE BROWNIES

3 oz (75g) margarine
2 oz (50g) cooking chocolate
2 beaten eggs
1 teaspoon (5ml) vanilla essence
6 oz (175g) caster sugar
2 oz (50g) chopped walnuts
3 oz (75g) plain flour
½ teaspoon (2.5ml) baking powder

Line a 7 inch (18cm) square tin with greaseproof paper. In a basin over a pan of hot water melt chocolate and margarine, mix well together and add eggs, vanilla, sugar and walnuts. Sieve together flour and baking powder and fold into mixture carefully. It should be quite runny. Pour into prepared tin. Bake at Gas Mark 4, 350F, 180C for 40 minutes. Cut into small squares.

CHOCOLATE STRIPS

4 oz (100g) flour
4 oz (100g) sultanas
2 oz (50g) margarine
2 oz (50g) chocolate
2 oz (50g) shelled walnuts
6 oz (175g) caster sugar
2 eggs
1 teaspoon (15ml) baking powder
1 tablespoon (15ml) milk
Caster sugar for top

Grate chocolate and dissolve in milk. Whisk caster sugar and eggs together until thick, add chocolate, then stir in sifted flour and baking powder. Add melted margarine, add fruit and chopped walnuts. Turn mixture into shallow Swiss roll tin. Dredge top with caster sugar. Bake Gas Mark 4, 350F, 180C for 20-25 minutes, until spongy. Cut into strips.

COCONUT SLICES

8 oz (225g) plain flour
1 teaspoon (15ml) baking
powder
4 oz (100g) margarine or
lard
1 egg
4 oz (100g) sugar
Pinch salt
Jam
Spread
3 oz (75g) coconut
3 oz (75g) sugar
1 egg

Rub fat into flour, add baking powder, and sugar. Make into a dough with egg. Roll out into neat oblong, place on greased tray or Swiss roll tin, spread with jam and cover with the coconut, 3 oz (75g) sugar and 1 egg. Bake at Gas Mark 4, 350F, 180C for 20-25 minutes. Cut into slices whilst hot (marzipan may be used as topping instead of coconut).

COCONUT BARS

4 oz (100g) desiccated coconut
4 oz (100g) caster sugar
4 oz (100g) glace cherries
1 egg
8 oz (225g) cooking chocolate

Line a Swiss roll tin with baking foil. Melt chocolate and pour over the foil, leave to set. Mix coconut, sugar and chopped cherries with the beaten egg. Spread mixture over the chocolate and bake about 10 minutes Gas Mark 5, 375F, 190C. Cut into bars when nearly cold.

COCONUT FINGERS

6 oz (175g) plain flour
3 oz (75g) margarine
2 oz (50g) sugar
½ teaspoon (2.5ml)
almond essence
4 tablespoons (60ml) jam
2 large eggs separated
4 oz (100g) caster sugar
1 tablespoon (15ml) self
raising flour
3 oz (75g) coconut

Rub margarine into flour until mixture resembles breadcrumbs. Stir in sugar, egg yolks and essence. Bind together to form a paste. Knead paste lightly until smooth then roll out to fit shallow 7x11 inch (18x28cm) tin. Cover the paste with jam. Whisk egg whites until stiff. Using a metal spoon fold in sugar, flour and coconut, then spread mixture over the jam. Bake at Gas Mark 4, 350F, 180C for 30 minutes. Allow to cool 5 minutes before cutting.

DATE BARS

6 oz (175g) rolled oats
6 oz (175g) flour
6 oz (175g) margarine
3 oz (75g) soft brown sugar
½ teaspoon (2.5ml)
bicarbonate of soda
Filling
8 oz (225g) dates
2 oz (50g) sugar
2-3 tablespoons (30-45ml) water

Make the filling by chopping the dates finely and stewing in the water with the sugar until a soft paste is formed. Rub the margarine into the flour, oats, and bicarbonate of soda, add sugar, the mixture should be like crumbs. Press half the mixture into a greased Swiss roll tin. Spread the date filling over, then the other half of the oat mixture. Press down well. Bake at Gas Mark 4, 350F, 180C for 40 minutes. Cut into fingers whilst hot. This recipe is equally good using mincemeat instead of dates.

DATE AND KRISPIE CHOCOLATE SLICE

2 oz (50g) margarine
8 oz (225g) dates
5 oz (150g) sugar
2 cups Rice Krispies
4 oz (100g) baking chocolate

Melt margarine in a pan with sugar and dates, add krispies and spread in a Swiss roll tin 12x8 inch (30x20cm). Cover with melted chocolate. Cut when set.

DATE SLICES

8 oz (225g) stoned dates
½ pint (275ml) water
1 teaspoon (5ml) vanilla
essence
4 oz (100g) self raising flour
1 teaspoon (5ml)
bicarbonate of soda
4 oz (100g) quick cooking
oats
6 oz (175g) caster sugar
4 oz (100g) butter or
margarine

Grease a Swiss roll tin. Chop dates and put in saucepan with water. Bring to boil, cook until soft, add essence. Sift flour with bicarb, stir in oats and sugar. Rub in fat lightly. Press half mixture evenly over tin. Press down to firm. Spread date mixture over and cover with remaining oat mixture, press lightly. Bake at Gas Mark 4, 350F, 180C for 20-30 minutes. Mark into bars and cool. Makes approximately 20 pieces.

DELIGHTFUL CRUNCH

4 oz (100g) butter
8 oz (225g) plain flour
2 tablespoons (30ml) icing
sugar
*Crumble together and
flatten into Swiss roll tin.*
Filling
2 eggs
6 oz (175g) caster sugar
3 oz (75g) chopped walnuts
3 oz (75g) coconut
3 oz (75g) chopped cherries

Beat eggs and sugar until almost stiff, stir in nuts, cherries and coconut. Place on top of base. Bake at Gas Mark 2, 300F, 150C for up to 50 minutes. Cut into bars before cold.

DATE AND WALNUT (NO PASTRY)

4 oz (100g) margarine
5 oz (150g) sugar
1 egg
3 oz (75g) self raising flour
2 oz (50g) walnuts
8 oz (225g) cooking dates

Cream margarine and sugar, add egg, flour, dates and nuts. Place mixture in a small square tin (or use double quantity for Swiss roll tin). Gas Mark 3, 325F, 170C for 45 minutes. Cut into squares.

DATE SQUARES

6 oz (175g) melted butter
8 oz (225g) dates
4 oz (100g) plain flour
6 oz (175g) porridge oats
6 oz (175g) soft brown
sugar
*Grated rind and juice 1
orange*

Grease a shallow 7 inch (18cm) square tin. Cut up dates and put into small saucepan with orange rind. Make up orange juice to about a quarter of a pint (150ml) with water and add to pan. Stir over a low heat until thick and soft. Put on one side to cool. Mix oats, flour and sugar together, add fat and mix with fork, to a crumbly texture. Press half mixture into tin, cover with date mixture and top with remaining crumb mixture. Press down lightly. Cook in centre oven Gas Mark 4, 350F, 180C for 30 minutes until golden brown. Remove from oven, leave to cool in tin. Cut into 16 squares.

EASY FLORENTINE SLICES

3 oz (75g) margarine
1 tablespoon (30ml)
golden syrup
8 oz (225g) Alpen
(breakfast cereal)
5 squares cooking chocolate
2 oz (50g) chopped dates
2 oz (50g) cherries

Melt margarine and golden syrup. Remove from heat. Stir in alpen, dates and cherries. Press into Swiss roll tin. Cover with melted chocolate.

FRUITY FLAPJACKS

4 oz (100g) margarine
2 oz (50g) demerara sugar
8 oz (225g) porridge oats
4 tablespoons (60ml)
golden syrup
2 oz (50g) raisins or
sultanas

Grease a shallow 7 inch (18cm) tin. Melt margarine, sugar and syrup together in a saucepan. Stir in fruit and oats. Press into tin. Bake in centre of oven Gas Mark 4, 350F, 180C for 30-35 minutes until golden brown. Cut into bars while warm, remove to wire rack.

FRENCH PASTY

12 oz (350g) self raising
flour
6 oz (175g) margarine
5 oz (150g) caster sugar
2 standard eggs
Milk to mix
Pinch salt
Raspberry jam

Sieve flour and salt together. Rub in margarine, add sugar, mix with beaten eggs and sufficient milk to form a rolling dough. Divide mixture into two pieces. Grease a 12x8 inch (30x20cm) Swiss roll tin and roll one half to fit base. Spread with jam, then roll other half and place on top of jam. Prick all over and bake in a fairly hot oven Gas Mark 6, 400F, 200C for about 15-20 minutes, until firm to the touch (Lemon curd may be used instead of jam).

FLAPJACKS

4 oz (100g) margarine
4 tablespoons (60ml)
golden syrup
3 oz (75g) sugar
8 oz (225g) rolled oats
¼ teaspoon (1.25ml) salt

Grease a 7½ inch (20cm) square shallow tin. Melt margarine and syrup in a pan over a low heat. Add sugar, oats and salt and mix thoroughly. Press into tin, bake at Gas Mark 3, 335F, 170C for 30-40 minutes until golden brown. Leave to cool 5 minutes then cut and place on wire tray.

GROUND RICE SQUARES

Raspberry jam
6 oz (175g) plain flour
3 oz (75g) lard and
margarine mixed
½ teaspoon (2.5ml) salt
Topping
4 oz (100g) margarine
4 oz (100g) caster sugar
2 eggs
4 oz (100g) ground rice

Sieve flour and salt together, rub in fat, mix with water to form a rolling dough. Line a 12x8 inch (30x20cm) Swiss roll tin with pastry and cover with raspberry jam. Cream margarine and sugar together, add eggs one at a time, beating well each time until light and fluffy, fold in ground rice (A little lemon rind or lemon juice may be added if desired). Spread mixture on top of jam. Bake in hot oven Gas Mark 7, 425F, 220C for 10 minutes reducing heat to Gas Mark 6, 400F, 200C for 10-15 minutes until top is firm to touch. Cool and cut into squares.

HONEY FLAPJACKS

4 oz (100g) margarine
2 dessertspoons (20ml)
honey
6 oz (175g) rolled oats
4 oz (100g) caster sugar

Put margarine with honey into saucepan, melt over gentle heat. Stir in sugar and rolled oats and mix well. Brush shallow baking tray 11½x7½ inch (29x19cm) with a little melted fat. Turn mixture into tin and spread evenly with a palette knife. Bake Gas Mark 4, 350F, 180C for about 20 minutes. Cool slightly and cut into squares.

PEPPERMINT BAKE WITH CHOCOLATE ICING

2 oz (50g) margarine
1 large egg
2 oz (50g) caster sugar
Pinch salt
5 oz (150g) plain flour
1 teaspoon (5ml) baking powder
1 oz (25g) peppermint creams
4 oz (125g) dessert chocolate

Beat margarine and sugar to a soft cream, add beaten egg and crumbled peppermint creams. Sift flour, baking powder and salt, add to rest of ingredients and mix well. Put into greased Swiss roll tin and bake at Gas Mark 5, 380F, 190C for 25 minutes. Whilst still warm spread with melted chocolate.

PEPPERMINT SLICES

4 oz (100g) margarine
1 dessertspoon (10ml) cocoa
Pinch salt
4 oz (100g) brown sugar
5 oz (150g) self raising flour
4 handfuls crushed cornflakes
Icing
green colouring
8 oz (225g) icing sugar
½ teaspoon (2.5ml) peppermint essence
Water to mix
2 small squares cooking chocolate

Put margarine in pan with sugar, melt over gentle heat, add crushed cornflakes, sift the dry ingredients into the pan and mix together thoroughly. Brush Swiss roll tin with melted fat, spread the mixture evenly in the tin and flatten the surface with a palette knife. Bake at Gas Mark 4, 350F, 180C for 25 minutes. Whilst still hot cut into squares or slices, allow to cool in tin. Mix the icing and put a spoonful in centre of each slice. Grate a little chocolate onto the icing whilst still wet.

PRALINE BARS

8 oz (225g) digestive biscuits
4 oz (100g) margarine
1 tablespoon (15ml) syrup
4 oz (100g) cooking chocolate
Plus 5 squares cooking chocolate
1 dessertspoon (10ml) sugar

Melt margarine, syrup and 100g chocolate in large basin over a pan of hot water. Stir in biscuit crumbs. Press into greased Swiss roll tin and leave 24 hours. Cover with melted squares of chocolate and cut into fingers when set.

RICE KRISPIE CRUNCH

4 oz (100g) margarine
2 oz (50g) creamy toffee
4 oz (100g) Rice Krispies
3 oz (75g) icing sugar

Put margarine and toffee into saucepan and heat slowly, stirring together as they melt. When toffee completely melted stir in Rice Krispies until they are thoroughly coated. Press mixture into a Swiss roll tin 13x9 inch (33x23cm) and leave to set. When set mix icing sugar with sufficient water to form a runny consistency and trickle this over. Leave icing to set then cut into 12 squares and cut each square into 2 triangles to make 24 pieces.

RICH JAM SHORTIES

4 oz (100g) plain flour
4 oz (100g) self raising flour
1 egg
4 oz (100g) sugar
4 oz (100g) margarine
Jam

Rub margarine into flour and mix in rest of dry ingredients, bind with beaten egg. Line Swiss roll tin with half pastry mixture, spread evenly with jam (plum jam is recommended) cover with remaining pastry. Bake at Gas Mark 4, 350F, 180C for 25 minutes.

FLAPJACK

4 oz (125g) sugar
4 oz (125g) butter or
margarine
4 oz (125g) rolled oats

Cream butter and sugar well, add oats. Press into a well greased Swiss roll tin. Bake in moderate oven, Gas Mark 4, 350F. 180C, until golden brown. Before it cools cut into squares.

CHOCOLATE ORANGE SHORTCAKE

8 oz (225g) margarine
6 oz (175g) caster sugar
1 orange, rind and juice
12 oz (350g) plain flour
½ oz (10g) baking
powder
4 oz (125g) chocolate

Cream together margarine and sugar, add orange rind and juice (zest only finely grated). Stir in sieved flour, place into greased large Swiss roll tin, sprinkle with flour and press down. Bake for approximately 30 minutes at Gas Mark 4, 350F, 180C. Cool and coat with melted chocolate, cut into fingers.

JIFFY FRUIT FINGERS

4 oz (100g) margarine
4 oz (100g) porridge oats
2 oz (50g) cherries
4 oz (100g) sultanas
2 oz (50g) chocolate chips
3 oz (75g) coconut
1 large tin condensed milk

Melt margarine in a large Swiss roll tin. When melted sprinkle oats on top, then cherries, sultanas and chocolate chips on top of oats, then coconut over them, and lastly condensed milk all over coconut. Cook in moderate oven at Gas Mark 4, 350F, 180C for 25-30 minutes, or until golden brown.

GIPSY CRUNCH

4 oz (100g) margarine
4 oz (100g)
marshmallows
4 oz (100g) toffee
4 oz (100g) Rice Krispies

Melt margarine, toffee and marshmallows in a pan — do not boil. Add Rice Krispies, mix well. Put in large Swiss roll tin and cover with chocolate, leave to set.

Chapter Thirteen

Cakes and Icings

YUM YUM CAKE

3 oz (75g) margarine
6 oz (175g) self raising
flour
2½ oz (60g) sugar
1 teaspoon baking powder
2 egg yolks
Milk to mix
Vanilla essence
Filling
2 egg whites
3 oz (75g) sugar
2 oz (50g) chopped
walnuts
2 oz (50g) cherries

Rub fat into flour and other dry ingredients. Mix with egg yolks and a drop of milk. Roll out on to a greased tray. For the filling: beat the egg whites until stiff and add the other ingredients. Spread this on to the rolled out mixture and bake in a moderate oven Gas Mark 3, 325F, 160C for approximately 30 minutes.

BOILED FRUIT CAKE

1 lb (450g) dried mixed
fruit
5½ oz (160g) margarine
5½ oz (160g) demerara
sugar
11 oz (300g) self raising
flour
¼ pint (125ml) water
2 eggs beaten with ¼ pint
(125ml) milk
3 oz (75g) chopped glacé
cherries

Place fruit, sugar, margarine and water in a large pan. Bring to the boil, stirring all the time, reduce heat and simmer for 20-25 minutes. Allow to cool. Beat the eggs with the milk, add flour, eggs, and cherries to the mixture in the pan, a little at a time until all is absorbed. Grease and line an 8 inch loose bottomed tin, pour in the mixture and bake for 1½-2 hours, at Gas Mark 2, 300F, or 150C.

BIRTHDAY OR CHRISTMAS CAKE

For 2lb Cake
5 oz (150g) butter
5 oz (150g) caster sugar
3 eggs
5 oz (150g) sifted plain
flour
5 oz (150g) currants
*Juice of half a lemon and
half an orange sprinkled
over washed and dried fruit*
5 oz (150g) sultanas
5 oz (150g) stoned or
seedless raisins
1 oz (25g) mixed peel

For 3½ lb Cake
8 oz (225g) butter
8 oz (225g) caster sugar
5 eggs
8 oz (225g) sifted plain
flour
8 oz (225g) currants
*Juice of 1 lemon and 1
orange sprinkled over
washed and dried fruit*
8 oz (225g) sultanas
8 oz (225g) stoned or
seedless raisins
2 oz (50g) mixed peel

Grease and line cake tin, (for 2 lb cake 6", for 3½ lb cake 7"). Preheat oven to Gas Mark 2, 300F, 150C. Cream the butter and sugar thoroughly, and add the beaten egg a little at a time. Fold in half the sieved flour. Add dried fruit and peel, (using the hand, evenly but lightly), finally fold in the remaining flour. Put into tin and bake for 2 hours 45 minutes (3 hours for 3½ lb). Store in airtight tin. The flavour can be improved by painting the sides and base once a week with rum.

FRESH LEMON CAKE

4 oz (125g) margarine
1 level teaspoon (5ml)
baking powder
6 oz (175g) self raising
flour
6 oz (175g) caster sugar
2 eggs
4 tablespoons (60ml) milk
Finely grated rind of lemon
Topping
Juice of 1 lemon
4 oz (125g) caster sugar.

Grease and line cake tin. Cream fat and sugar, add eggs, flour, lemon rind and milk. Mix well. Put into tin smooth top and bake for approximately 50 minutes at Gas Mark 4, 350F, or 180C. Mix sugar and lemon juice for topping and pour over cake as soon as it comes out of the oven. Leave in tin until completely cold. Approximately 8 inch round tin or 2 lb loaf tin.

MADEIRA CAKE

8 oz (225g) self raising
flour
6 oz (175g) butter
7 oz (200g) caster sugar
4 eggs
Finely grated rind of 1
lemon
A strip of lemon citron
peel, washed and dried
(optional)

Heat the oven to Gas Mark 4, 350F, 180C. Grease and line a 7 inch (18cm) round cake tin. Measure all the ingredients except the peel, into a bowl and beat well or use a food processor. Spread the mixture in the prepared tin and level. Bake for 30 minutes until set, then carefully lift the peel on to the cake. Reduce the oven temperature to Gas Mark 3, 325F, 160C, and cook for a further hour. (Total cooking time, 1 hour 30 minutes). The cake should be shrinking away slightly from the sides of the tin and be pale golden in colour.

PINEAPPLE CAKE

6 oz (175g) brown sugar
4 oz (125g) butter
2 eggs
1 small tin crushed
pineapple (strained and
sieved)
12 oz (350g) mixed fruit
6 oz (175g) cherries
6 oz (175g) plain flour

Put all ingredients except eggs and flour in a pan and boil for 5-6 minutes. When cool add beaten egg and shake in flour. Put in round or square 8 inch tin and bake in low oven Gas Mark 2, 300F, or 155C.

SIMNEL CAKE

8 oz (225g) butter
12 oz (350g) flour
12 oz (350g) currants
3 eggs
2 lemons
1 lb (450g) caster sugar
4 oz (125g) citron peel
½ teaspoonful allspice
1 lb (450g) ground
almonds
2 tablespoons brandy

Cream 6 oz (175g) of the butter with 6 oz (175g) of the sugar, beat the yolks of the eggs with a little milk, then add flour and eggs alternately to the creamed mixture. Cut the citron peel into small pieces and add to the mixture along with grated rind of the lemons, spice, currants, brandy, and whites of eggs whipped. In a separate basin melt 2 oz (50g) of butter, then add the almonds and remainder of sugar, juice of the lemons, and two eggs. Grease and line an 8 inch cake tin, put in half the cake mixture, then half the almond mixture, then the remainder of the cake mixture. Bake in a moderate oven Gas Mark 4, 350F, or 180C for approximately 1½ hours. Take out of oven, spread remainder of almond mixture on top, return to oven and bake for approximately 35 minutes longer.

VICTORIA SANDWICH

4 oz (125g) margarine or butter
2 eggs
4 oz (125g) caster sugar
4 oz (125g) self raising flour (or 4oz (125g) plain flour and rounded teaspoon baking powder)

Cream fat and sugar, add beaten eggs gradually. Sieve flour and fold into mixture. Line bottom of a well greased 7 inch (approx.) cake tin or 2x8 inch sandwich tins. Bake at 325-350F, or 165-180C for 25-30 minutes in two tins or 40-45 minutes in one tin.

VARIATIONS

This mixture will make 20 small buns and with the additions of 1½ oz currants for Queen cakes.

Chocolate | Substitute 1 oz (25g) flour with 1 tablespoon cocoa and add a little vanilla essence.

Coffee | Add 1 teaspoon coffee essence or coffee water.

Walnut | 2 oz (50g) walnuts chopped, half a teaspoon of vanilla.

Orange | Rind of half an orange, use juice to make glacé icing for tops.

Lemon | Add finely grated rind of a lemon, use juice to make glacé icing for tops.

Coconut | Add 2 oz (50g) coconut.

CHERRY AND ALMOND CAKE

4 oz (125g) butter
4 oz (125g) sugar
2 eggs
Salt
7 oz (200g) flour
1 teaspoon baking powder
2 oz (50g) ground almonds
2 oz (50g) glacé cherries
Little milk to mix

Grease and line a 7 inch cake tin. Cream butter and sugar. Beat eggs with a pinch of salt and add gradually to the creamed mixture. Add flour, baking powder and ground almonds gradually, also cherries cut in half and lightly floured. Add milk as required to make a fairly moist mixture. Bake in a slow to moderate oven at Gas Mark 2, 300F, 150C for 1 hour 15-30 minutes. Can be covered with white icing and decorated with cherries and almonds when cold.

CHOCOLATE ORANGE DRIZZLE CAKE

6 oz (175g) luxury margarine
6 oz (175g) self raising flour
Finely grated rind of 2 oranges
6 oz (175g) caster sugar
3 eggs
2 tablespoons cold milk
Orange Syrup
4 oz (100g) caster sugar, dissolved in the juice of 2 oranges
Chocolate Topping
4 oz (100g) block plain chocolate
½ oz (12g) butter

Grease a 2 lb loaf tin and line with paper. Cream sugar and margarine until soft, beat in eggs one at a time. Fold in sifted flour, add the milk, and finely grated orange rind. Turn mixture into prepared tin and bake in a moderate oven, Gas Mark 3, 325F, 160C for one hour until well risen and brown. Turn cake out to cool and when almost cold make slits across the top of the cake with a fork and drizzle in the orange syrup so that it soaks in to the cake. Break chocolate into small pieces and place in a bowl with butter and allow to melt over gently steaming water, mix well and use immediately. Spread chocolate topping in whirls on top of the cake (cuts into 8-10 pieces).

COCONUT CAKE

6 oz (175g) self raising flour
4 oz (125g) butter
2 eggs
2 tablespoons milk
2 tablespoons coconut
5 oz (150g) caster sugar
Pinch of salt

Prepare 7 inch cake tin. Cream butter and sugar, add eggs one at a time and beat well. Mix flour and coconut together before adding to above mixture. Add milk gradually. Bake at Gas Mark 3, 325F, 160C middle shelf for one hour. Sprinkle a little coconut on cake before putting in the oven.

DUNDEE CAKE

12 oz (350g) self raising flour
8 oz (225g) butter
8 oz (225g) soft brown sugar
1 lb (450g) currants
12 oz (350g) sultanas
4 oz (125g) glacé cherries
4 oz (125g) ground almonds
1 tablespoon marmalade
5 eggs
Wine glass of rum or brandy
Blanched almonds for top

Cream butter and sugar, add eggs and flour alternately. Add fruit and marmalade and ground almonds and lastly add rum and brandy. Put into greased cake tin and arrange nuts on top and bake in oven, Gas Mark 3, 325F, 160C, and then reduce after 30 minutes to Gas Mark 2, 300F, 150C.

ORANGE CAKE

6 oz (175g) margarine
Rind and juice of 1 orange
6 oz (175g) sugar
3 eggs
8 oz (225g) self raising flour

Cream the margarine together with grated orange rind. Add the sugar and beat until white. Gradually beat in the eggs. Lightly fold in the flour together with orange juice to give a soft dropping consistency. Bake in two greased sandwich tins, 8 inch or 9 inch diameter for 25-30 minutes at Gas Mark 3, 325F, 160C, or bake in a deep 7 inch tin for one hour, lowering the heat if necessary.

PARADISE CAKE

12 oz (350g) sultanas
8 oz (225g) cherries (¼ lb green, ¼ lb red)
6 oz (175g) glacé pineapple
2 oz (50g) glacé ginger
2 oz (50g) angelica
2 oz (50g) mixed peel
2 oz (50g) walnuts
8 oz (225g) plain flour
4 oz (125g) self raising flour
5 eggs
8 oz (225g) sugar
12 oz (350g) margarine or butter
Rind and juice of 1 lemon
8 tablespoons milk or sherry

Prepare a 9 inch cake tin. Cream together sugar and fat and gradually add the beaten eggs. Add the flour together with the rest of the ingredients and mix together lightly. Bake in moderate oven Gas Mark 3, 325F, 160C for the first 1 hour approx. Reduce the heat to Gas Mark 2, 300F, 150C for a further 2 hours approx.

YORKSHIRE PARKIN

8 oz (225g) medium oatmeal
4 oz (125g) plain flour
1 level teaspoon baking powder
or 4 oz (125g) self raising flour
4 oz (125g) moist brown sugar
3 oz (75g) margarine
8 oz (225g) golden syrup
1 tablespoon black treacle
⅓ pint (200ml) milk
1½ level teaspoons ground ginger

Melt the margarine in the syrup and treacle and add to the dry ingredients. Add the milk, pour the mixture into a lined 8 inch square baking tin. Bake at Gas Mark 3, 325F, 160C for 2 hours.

RICE CAKE

4 oz (125g) margarine
4 oz (125g) sugar
3 oz (75g) self raising
flour
1 tablespoon ground
almonds
2 eggs
1 oz ground rice

Cream margarine and sugar, add eggs, then lightly fold in dry ingredients, mix well together, put into well greased 1 lb loaf tin. Bake in moderate oven for about 1 hour 15 minutes at Gas Mark 3, 325F, 160C.

FATLESS SPONGE CAKE

3 eggs at room temperature
4½ oz caster sugar
3 oz (75g) plain flour

Prepare 8 inch tin, greased, base lined. Whisk eggs and sugar until very thick and leaves a trail. Fold in sieved flour. Pour into tin. Bake in centre of oven at Gas Mark 3, 300F, 150C, for approximately 40-50 minutes.

CHERRY LOAF

5 oz (150g) margarine or
butter
5 oz (150g) sugar
2 eggs
4 oz (125g) cherries
8 oz (225g) plain flour
Milk to mix
A little sugar to sprinkle on
the top and a few cut
cherries
½ level teaspoon baking
powder

Cream the butter and sugar and add the well beaten eggs. Cream well, then mix in the flour and baking powder, stirring in a little milk. Put mixture into greased 2 lb loaf tin and sprinkle on cut cherries and sugar. Bake in a moderate oven, Gas Mark 3 to 4 or 350-375F, 160-180C, for 1 hour 30 minutes. Turn down oven if necessary.

COCONUT LOAF

4 oz (100g) margarine
4 oz (100g) caster sugar
2 large eggs
3 oz (75g) self raising
flour
2 oz (50g) coconut
2 oz (50g) ground
almonds

Cream the margarine and sugar. Beat in the eggs, and fold in the dry ingredients. Bake in a 1 lb loaf tin for 40 minutes at Gas Mark 3, 325F, 160C.

LEMON CURD LOAF

2 oz (50g) butter
2 oz (50g) caster sugar
1 egg
1 tablespoon of lemon curd
3 oz (75g) self raising
flour

Cream the butter and sugar, add the egg and lemon curd. Fold in the flour. Bake in a 1 lb loaf tin for 40 minutes at Gas Mark 3, 325F, 160C.

ALMOND PASTE

½ lb (225g) ground almonds
¼ lb (125g) caster sugar
¼ lb (125g) icing sugar
1 beaten egg
2 teaspoons lemon juice
¼ teaspoon almond essence

Mix all dry ingredients together and mix to a stiff paste with beaten egg and flavourings. This amount will cover top and sides of 7-8 inch round cake.

BUTTER CREAM

4 oz (125g) butter or margarine
6 oz (175g) to 8 oz (225g) sieved icing sugar

Cream butter until soft, beat in sugar gradually, then beat until light and fluffy adding a little milk for good spreading.

VARIATIONS

Coffee 2-3 teaspoons coffee essence or 2 teaspoons instant coffee in 1 tablespoon hot water.

Chocolate 1 level tablespoon cocoa

Lemon 1-2 tablespoons lemon curd, omit milk

Orange 1 tablespoon orange juice, omit milk.

CHOCOLATE FUDGE ICING

5 oz (150g) icing sugar
1 dessertspoon cocoa
2 oz (50g) margarine or butter
2 dessertspoons water

Put all the ingredients in a basin and heat over a pan of hot water, stirring all the time, until butter has melted and all is well blended. Use immediately. Sufficient to cover top of two 8 inch cakes.

FONDANT ICING

1 lb (450g) icing sugar
1 teaspoon glycerine
1 dessertspoon liquid glucose
1 egg white

Place sieved sugar in a bowl. Make a well in the centre, add egg white, glucose and glycerine. Beat the mixture gradually drawing in icing sugar. Knead until smooth. Roll out to size required and place over cake.

ROYAL ICING

1 lb (450g) sieved icing sugar
2 egg whites
2 teaspoons glycerine

Lightly beat egg whites, add half of the icing sugar, beat with wooden spoon for about 10 minutes and add remaining sugar and glycerine. Beat for 4-5 minutes more.

Chapter Fourteen

Biscuits

COFFEE CRISPS

2 oz (50g) walnuts
2 rounded teaspoons
instant coffee
2 teaspoons very hot water
4 oz (125g) margarine
4 oz (125g) caster sugar
6 oz (175g) self raising
flour

Take 1½ oz of walnuts and put in a polythene bag, crush them finely with a rolling pin. Dissolve coffee in hot water. Cream margarine and sugar. Mix in dissolved coffee and crushed walnuts. Fold in sieved flour, blend well and using hands form small balls of the mixture and put on a greased baking sheet, well apart. Flatten slightly and using rest of walnuts broken up put a piece on the top of each biscuit. Bake in a moderate oven Gas Mark 4, 350F or 180C for 15-20 minutes. When quite cold store in an airtight tin.

PEANUT BISCUITS

6 oz (175g) plain flour
¾ teaspoon bicarbonate of
soda
4 oz (125g) soft
margarine
3 oz (75g) caster sugar
3 oz (75g) soft brown
sugar
½ teaspoon baking powder
¼ teaspoon salt
3 tablespoons (45ml)
peanut butter
1 egg

Place all ingredients together in a bowl and beat until smooth. Form into a roll. Wrap roll in foil and chill in fridge or freezer. Slice roll thinly and place well apart on greased baking tray. Bake at Gas Mark 5, 375F, 190C, for 7-10 minutes.

SNAPPED OATS

5 oz (150g) butter or margarine
1 tablespoon syrup
3 oz (75g) plain flour
6 oz (175g) rolled oats
½ teaspoon bicarbonate of soda, dissolved in 2 tablespoons of HOT water
8 oz (225g) sugar

Preheat oven to Gas Mark 4, 350F, 180C, grease baking trays. Melt butter, sugar and syrup in pan over a low heat. Stir in dry ingredients and then bicarbonate of soda. Mix thoroughly, place teaspoonful of mixture well apart on prepared trays. Bake about 15 minutes until golden brown.

SWEDISH DREAMS

4 oz (125g) margarine
2 oz (50g) lard
2 oz (50g) sugar
2 oz (50g) custard powder
6 oz (175g) self raising flour
A little milk

Cream together margarine, lard and sugar. Fold in flour and custard powder with a little milk. Roll into small balls in sugar. Bake for 30 minutes until golden brown at Gas Mark 4, 350F, 180C.

VIENNESE FINGERS

4 oz (125g) flour
4 oz (125g) butter
1 oz (25g) icing sugar
Melted chocolate
Filling
3 oz (75g) butter
5 oz (150g) icing sugar, sifted
1 oz (25g) cocoa powder

Cream the butter and sugar. Add flour, and mix well. Put the mixture into a piping bag with a large star nozzle, and pipe three inch lengths onto a greased baking sheet. Bake for 10 minutes at Gas Mark 4, 350F, or 180C. Filling: Beat all the ingredients together until thick and creamy. When cool, sandwich together with the filling, and dip the ends in the melted chocolate.

AFGHANS

6 oz (175g) butter
4 oz (100g) caster sugar
5 oz (150g) plain flour
2 level tablespoons (30ml)
cocoa
2 oz (50g) crushed
cornflakes
Melted chocolate for icing

Cream fat and sugar, add dry ingredients, mix altogether thoroughly and put on to a baking sheet a small spoonful flattening with a fork and leaving room to spread. Bake in a moderate oven Gas Mark 4, 350F, 180C for 15 minutes and when cool coat with melted chocolate.

ALMOND MACAROONS

2 large egg whites
4 oz (100g) ground
almonds
6 oz (175g) caster sugar
1 oz (25g) ground rice
Few drops almond essence
8 almonds blanched

Line trays with rice paper or household parchment. Put 1 teaspoon (5ml) egg white to one side for glazing. Whisk remaining egg white until it forms soft peaks. Fold in ground almonds, sugar, ground rice and almond essence and mix well. Put heaped teaspoons of mixture on to the trays and smooth with the back of a spoon, top with half-almonds and brush with egg white. Bake for 25-30 minutes at Gas Mark 2, 300F, 150C.

ALMOND BISCUITS (PLAIN)

6 oz (175g) self raising
flour
3 oz (75g) caster sugar
2 oz (50g) ground
almonds
5 oz (150g) margarine
Pinch salt
¼ teaspoon (1.25ml) almond
essence
Blanched almonds

Mix together dry ingredients, rub in margarine, add essence and knead well. Roll out ¼ inch (5mm) thick and cut into rounds, with half blanched almond on each. Bake in moderate oven Gas Mark 3, 325F, 170C for about 15 minutes.

BRANDY SNAP

4 oz (100g) butter
4 oz (100g) sugar
4 oz (100g) golden syrup
3 oz (75g) flour
Little ground ginger
Pinch salt

Prepare moderate oven Gas Mark 4, 350F, 180C. Measure golden syrup carefully, place in small saucepan together with butter and sugar. Heat slowly until butter has melted, remove from heat. Sift flour, ginger and salt together and stir into saucepan with rest of ingredients. Leave to become quite cold. Place small teaspoonful of mixture on a greased baking sheet, well apart to allow for spreading and bake 8-14 minutes until deep golden brown. Have ready a wooden spoon and whilst brandy snap still hot, curl round handle. Leave to cool and store in an airtight tin (Brandy snap can be filled with whipped cream before serving).

BACHELOR'S BUTTONS

5 oz (150g) self raising flour
3 oz (75g) sugar
2 oz (50g) butter
1 egg
Jam or lemon curd

Rub flour, butter and sugar together, add beaten egg. Roll into walnut sized balls. Dip in sugar, make hole in centre of ball with little finger, put in a dab of jam or lemon curd. Bake on a greased baking sheet in a slow oven Gas Mark 2, 300F, 150C for 15 minutes. Makes about 16.

BOURBON BISCUITS

4 oz (100g) caster sugar
6 oz (175g) plain flour
4 oz (100g) butter or
margarine
2 level tablespoons (30ml)
cocoa
2 oz (50g) custard powder
1 small egg
Filling
1 ½ oz (40g) butter
2 oz (50g) sifted icing
sugar
2 level dessertspoons
(20ml) powdered drinking
chocolate
1 teaspoon (5ml) coffee
essence

Beat sugar and butter to a soft cream. Sift together flour, custard powder and cocoa. Beat the egg lightly and add to the creamed mixture with dry ingredients. Work mixture into rather a stiff dough. Roll out to almost ¼ inch (5mm) thickness and cut into fingers 3x1 inch (8x3cm). Prick each down centre and sprinkle lightly with sugar. Bake on slightly greased trays Gas Mark 4, 350F, 180C for 10-12 minutes. Cool on wire tray and sandwich together with filling.

BUTTERSCOTCH WALNUTS

4 oz (100g) margarine
6 oz (175g) self raising
flour
1 oz (25g) cornflakes
4 oz (100g) brown sugar
1 tablespoon (15ml)
golden syrup
Halves walnuts

Put margarine, sugar and syrup into a bowl and beat for 1 minute. Add flour and cornflakes and knead very thoroughly. Roll out into 24 small balls, flatten slightly. Put halved walnuts on top and place on lightly greased baking sheets allowing room to spread. Bake for 15 minutes at Gas Mark 4, 350F, 180C. Cool on the tins.

COCONUT LOGS

8 oz (225g) cooking
chocolate
6 oz (175g) margarine or
butter
8 oz (225g) icing sugar
8 oz (225g) coconut
1 teaspoon (5ml) vanilla
essence ·

Cream margarine and sugar, add vanilla essence and coconut. Mould well and leave until set. Roll into bars and dip into warm melted chocolate. Place on greaseproof paper until cold before storing in a tin. (Sugar tongs are very useful for the dipping process.)

CHERRY SHORTBREAD

4 oz (100g) butter
2 oz (50g) caster sugar
2 oz (50g) cornflour
1 oz (25g) desiccated
coconut
2 oz (50g) chopped cherries
4 oz (100g) plain flour

Cream sugar and butter until light. Mix in rest of ingredients. Press into a 7 inch (18cm) square shallow tin and smooth the surface. Bake in a preheated oven at Gas Mark 3, 325F, 170C for 25-30 minutes. Cut into fingers and sprinkle with sugar. Allow to cool in tin.

CRUNCHIES

2 oz (50g) lard
2 oz (50g) margarine
3 oz (75g) sugar
1 tablespoon (15ml)
golden syrup
3 teaspoons (15ml) boiling
water
Few drops vanilla essence
4 oz (100g) self raising
flour
2 oz (50g) rolled oats

Cream fats and sugar, add syrup, boiling water and vanilla. Stir in flour and oats, mix well. Roll into small balls and place on a well greased baking sheet. Bake at Gas Mark 3, 325F, 170C for 15-20 minutes.

CATS' TONGUES

Vanilla or lemon essence
Pinch salt
2 oz (50g) butter
2 oz (50g) caster sugar
2 oz (50g) plain flour
2 egg whites

Warm butter in a basin over hot water until soft but not oily. Beat lightly with a fork, gradually add sugar, beating all the time until very light. Beat in unwhisked egg whites a little at a time. Sift the flour with a pinch of salt and fold into the mixture gently. Flavour with lemon rind or vanilla essence. Put into forcing bag half-inch (1cm) plain nozzle and pipe in 2 inch (5cm) lengths on greased floured baking sheets. Allow room to spread. Bake at Gas Mark 5, 375F, 190C for 10 minutes until golden brown round edges. Good with stewed fruit or ice cream.

CUSTARD CREAMS

6 oz (175g) flour
3 oz (75g) caster sugar
4 oz (100g) margarine
2 tablespoons (30ml)
custard powder
Pinch salt
1 teaspoon (5ml) baking
powder
1 egg

Rub fat into dry ingredients and mix to a smooth paste with beaten egg. Cut into rounds and bake in a moderate oven Gas Mark 4, 350F, 180C until pale brown, approximately 15 minutes. Can be sandwiched together with butter icing and the paste is good made into jam tarts.

COCONUT BISCUITS

8 oz (225g) plain flour
8 oz (225g) sugar
8 oz (225g) coconut
8 oz (225g) margarine
2 tablespoons (30ml) milk

Rub the margarine into dry ingredients and mix with milk to stiff dough. Roll out thinly and cut into shapes with cutter. Bake in slow oven until pale fawn colour Gas Mark 2, 300F, 150C for 12-15 minutes.

COCONUT MACAROONS

2 egg whites
4 oz (100g) caster sugar
5 oz (150g) desiccated coconut
1 level dessertspoon (15ml) cornflour
16 blanched almond halves
Rice paper

Put the rice paper on to baking trays. Whisk the egg whites until they are just frothy but not stiff. Using a metal spoon stir in cornflour, caster sugar, and coconut and bind ingredients together. Place heaped teaspoonful of the mixture on the rice paper allowing a space between each as they spread slightly during cooking. Put a halved almond in the centre of each macaroon and bake centre shelf in oven Gas Mark 4, 250F, 180C for 20 minutes until tinged with golden brown. Tear off the surplus rice paper and leave to cool on a wire tray.

CRISPY ALMOND SHORTIES

6 oz (175g) flour
Pinch salt
2 oz (50g) ground rice
6 oz (175g) butter
2 oz (50g) caster sugar
2 oz (50g) chopped almonds

Place flour, salt, ground rice and sugar in bowl, rub in butter until a firm dough is formed. Roll out and cut into rounds. Sprinkle with chopped almonds. Bake at Gas Mark 4, 350F, 180C for 12-15 minutes. Makes about 20.

EASTER BISCUITS

3 oz (75g) margarine
4 oz (100g) self raising flour
1 1/2 oz (40g) sugar
1 oz (25g) currants
Pinch ground cinnamon
Grated rind 1/4 lemon
1 egg yolk

Rub fat into flour, add sugar, currants, rind and cinnamon, mix with egg. Work on a board to remove cracks. Roll out thinly, cut with fluted cutter. Bake in a moderate oven for 10 minutes at Gas Mark 4, 350F, 180C.

FRENCH SHORTBREAD

4 oz (100g) butter
2 oz (50g) caster sugar
8 oz (225g) plain flour
1 teaspoon (5ml) baking powder
1 teaspoon (5ml) ginger
Topping
4 oz (100g) icing sugar
2 oz (50g) margarine
1 teaspoon (5ml) syrup
1 teaspoon (5ml) ground ginger

Cream butter and sugar until light. Mix in rest of ingredients. Press into shallow 7 inch (18cm) square tin and smooth the surface. Bake in preheated oven Gas Mark 3, 325F, 170C for 25-30 minutes. Topping: Heat in a pan sugar, margarine, syrup and ginger, but do NOT boil. Pour over shortbread whilst still hot. When almost set cut into squares or fingers.

FRUIT DROPS

4 oz (100g) margarine
4 oz (100g) sugar
2 tablespoons (30ml) golden syrup
7 oz (200g) self raising flour
1 oz (25g) sultanas
1 oz (25g) currants
1 egg
Pinch of salt

Beat the margarine and sugar to a cream, add the syrup and egg and beat very well. Add flour and fruit and mix until thick and smooth. Put heaped teaspoonfuls well apart on a greased tray and bake at Gas Mark 4, 350F, 180C for 20 minutes. Remove to cooling tray at once.

FLORENTINES

4 oz (100g) butter
3 oz (75g) caster sugar
2 oz (50g) peel
2 oz (50g) cherries
4 oz (100g) nuts
(almonds or walnuts)
2 tablespoons (30ml)
cream
6 oz (175g) dark chocolate

Melt butter and sugar in pan, bring to boil and boil for one minute. Chop cherries, nuts and peel, add cream. Mix well all together. Place spoonfuls on vegetable parchment well apart. Bake at Gas Mark 4, 350F, 180C for 10 minutes. When cool spread with melted chocolate.

GOLDEN GOODIES

2 oz (50g) butter
2 oz (50g) coconut
3 oz (75g) plain flour
4 oz (125g) soft brown
sugar
1 level teaspoon (5ml)
baking powder
1 egg
Vanilla essence
Good pinch of salt
Halves glacé cherries for the
tops

Put butter and sugar into saucepan and melt over low heat, take off and cool. Beat egg in small basin. Stir in coconut to mixture, add egg and vanilla. Sift in flour, baking powder and salt and stir well. Put teaspoonfuls of the mixture on a baking tray, leaving room to spread. Put a half cherry in the centre of each biscuit. Gas Mark 4, 350F, 180C. Bake about 10 minutes, changing tins round halfway. Leave to cool for 2 minutes before slipping onto wire rack. Makes about 22.

KING HAAKON BISCUITS

8 oz (225g) plain flour
8 oz (225g) margarine or
butter
4 oz (100g) icing sugar

Knead all ingredients together and roll into a long sausage shape. Leave in refrigerator until quite cold. With a sharp knife cut off thin slices and bake to a golden brown in moderate oven Gas Mark 5, 375F, 190C for 10 minutes. Uncooked freezes well.

GINGER NUTS

8 oz (225g) margarine
8 oz (225g) sugar
8 tablespoons (120ml)
warmed syrup
1 lb (450g) plain flour
1 teaspoon (5ml)
bicarbonate of soda
2 teaspoons (20ml) ground
ginger
Pinch salt

Melt fat, sugar and syrup. Mix dry ingredients and add to melted mixture to make a stiff dough. Roll into balls using about a teaspoon of mixture each and place on greased tray. Bake at Gas Mark 4, 350F, 180C for about 15 minutes.

LANCASHIRE NUTS

4 oz (100g) flour
4 oz (100g) butter or
margarine
4 oz (100g) sugar
½ teaspoon (2.5ml) baking
powder
4 oz (100g) cornflour
1 egg
Lemon curd

Beat butter and sugar to a cream, add beaten egg and flours sifted with baking powder alternately. Shape into small balls of an equal size. Flatten a little. Bake in moderate oven Gas Mark 5, 375F, 190C for 10-15 minutes. When cold put two together with lemon curd and dust with icing sugar or caster sugar.

LEMON SHORTBREAD

5 oz (150g) plain flour
2 oz (50g) fine semolina
4 oz (100g) butter or
margarine
2 oz (50g) sugar
Grated rind of lemon
Pinch of salt

Sieve flour, semolina and salt. Cream butter and sugar and add grated lemon rind and other dry ingredients. Knead lightly and roll out to ¼ inch (5mm) thick, cut into shapes and prick with fork. Bake on lightly greased tray in moderate oven Gas Mark 4, 350F, 180C for 30-35 minutes until golden. Sprinkle with caster sugar.

MELTING MOMENTS

2½ oz (70g) lard
1½ oz (40g) margarine
4 oz (100g) sugar
1 teaspoon (5ml) baking
powder
5 oz (150g) flour
Vanilla essence
Porridge oats
Cherries

Cream fat and sugar, add essence, flour and baking powder. With wet hands mould the mixture into balls, flatten and dip in porridge oats. Decorate with a cherry. Bake in a moderate oven Gas Mark 5, 375F, 190C for 15-20 minutes.

NEW ZEALAND BISCUITS

5 oz (150g) butter
4 oz (100g) caster sugar
3 oz (75g) rolled oats
2 oz (50g) desiccated
coconut
4 oz (100g) plain flour
1 tablespoon (15ml)
golden syrup
2 teaspoons (10ml)
bicarbonate of soda

Put syrup, butter and sugar into a pan and melt over a low heat. Stir in dry ingredients. Dissolve bicarb of soda in 1 tablespoon (15ml) hot water, add to the other ingredients and leave to cool. Roll into balls, place on greased baking trays leaving plenty of room to run out. Bake about 20 minutes until evenly browned Gas Mark 3, 335F, 170C.

OAT BISCUITS

8 oz (225g) rolled oats
6 oz (175g) soft
margarine
4 oz (100g) sugar
2 oz (50g) plain flour

Mix all ingredients together in a bowl . Roll out as thin as possible, cut into rounds. Bake Gas Mark 4, 350F, 180C for 20 minutes.

PARLIES

8 oz (225g) plain flour
2 teaspoons (10ml) ground ginger
4 oz (100g) dark soft brown sugar
4 tablespoons (60ml) black treacle
4 oz (100g) margarine

Sift flour and ginger into a bowl; add brown sugar. Measure black treacle carefully, levelling off spoon with a knife and making sure there is none on undersides of spoon: place in a saucepan, add margarine; heat, stirring occasionally until melted. Remove from heat, stir into flour mixture. Mix well. Turn out onto lightly floured board and knead lightly. Roll out about ¼ inch (5mm) thick. Cut into rounds with a 2 inch (5cm) plain cutter. Bake at Gas Mark 4, 350F, 180C for 12-15 minutes.

QUAKER OATS BISCUITS

5 oz (150g) self raising flour
5 oz (150g) Quaker Oats
Pinch salt
4 oz (125g) margarine
2 oz (50g) sugar
2 tablespoons (30ml) milk

Mix together dry ingredients, rub in margarine and mix with milk to make a stiff paste. Roll out and cut into rounds. Place on greased baking sheet Gas Mark 4, 350F, 180C for 15-20 minutes.

RICE BISCUITS

4 oz (125g) self raising flour
4 oz (125g) sugar
4 oz (125g) ground rice
4 oz (125g) butter or margarine
1 oz (25g) cornflour
1 oz (25g) coconut
Walnut of lard
1 egg
Pinch of salt
2 or 3 drops vanilla essence

Mix all the dry ingredients, rub in the fats, beat egg, add flavouring and mix to a stiff dough. Roll out and cut into rounds with cutter. Bake in a fairly hot oven Gas Mark 6, 400F, 200C for 10-15 minutes until a pale golden brown. Cool on a wire tray.

SABLE PASTE

6 oz (175g) butter
3 oz (75g) sugar
1 egg
8 oz (225g) plain flour
3 oz (75g) ground
almonds
1 teaspoon (5ml) baking
powder

Mix flour, ground almonds and baking powder together. Beat butter and sugar to a soft cream, add egg and flour mixture. Mix well together to a soft mixture. Pipe into shapes on a greased tin. Decorate with cherries, almonds etc. Bake at Gas Mark 5, 375F, 190C for 30 minutes until a pale brown.

TUILES A L'ORANGE

2 small eggs
2 oz (50g) margarine
4 oz (100g) sugar
2 oz (50g) flour
Grated orange rind or
orange flavouring

Melt the margarine. Beat the eggs and sugar thoroughly. Add melted margarine and flour by degrees and flavouring. Spread out in teaspoonfuls on a well greased baking sheet and bake in a moderate oven Gas Mark 4, 350F, 180C for 8-12 minutes. Take off at once and curl slightly by rolling on a greased rolling pin. Put at once into an airtight tin if not using immediately.

WALNUT DROPS

4 oz (100g) sugar
2 oz (50g) lard
4 oz (100g) margarine
6 oz (175g) self raising
flour
1 egg
2 oz (50g) chopped
walnuts
A few cornflakes

Cream the sugar and fats together, add flour and beaten egg alternately and lastly add the nuts. Mix well and roll dessertspoonfuls in cornflakes. Bake at Gas Mark 4, 350F, 180C for 25 minutes.

WARWICKSHIRE CHOCOLATE BISCUITS

3 oz (75g) margarine
2 oz (50g) soft brown sugar
4 oz (100g) self raising flour
1 oz (25g) crushed cornflakes
2 teaspoons (10ml) cocoa or drinking chocolate
Vanilla essence
Pinch of salt

Cream margarine, and sugar together. Stir in cocoa, salt and vanilla essence. Mix well and beat in flour and cornflakes gradually. Knead well, shape into walnut sized balls and flatten. Bake at Gas Mark 3, 325F, 170C for 5 minutes approximately.

YO YO'S

6 oz (175g) margarine
6 oz (175g) self raising flour
2 oz (50g) custard powder
2 oz (50g) icing sugar
Pinch of salt
Butter cream
Pink colouring
4 oz (100g) icing sugar
2 oz (50g) butter

Cream margarine, sieve in flour, custard powder and icing sugar and salt. Mix well together. Roll the mixture into walnut size balls, flatten slightly. Bake at Gas Mark 4, 350F, 180C for about 15 minutes. Cream butter and icing sugar well together, add a few drops of pink colouring. When cold sandwich two together with butter cream.

Index

The WI movement began in Britain more than 80 years ago with the aim of enriching the lives of women living in remote rural areas and increasing their opportunities for education. Conditions have changed over these eight decades with improved networks of communication and transport. The WI never resists changes but has done much to guide their direction.

We are friendly, go ahead, like-minded women, who derive enormous satisfaction from all the movement has to offer. The list is long — you can make friends, have fun and companionship, visit new places, develop new skills, take part in community services, fight local campaigns, become a WI market producer, and play an active role in an organisation which has a national voice.

For more information about a WI near you write to the National Federation of Women's Institutes, 104 New Kings Road, London SW6 4LY or telephone 0171 371 9300.